THE LIE

AND

THE POWER OF CREATION

ALEXANDER ATLESKI

iUniverse, Inc.
Bloomington

The Lie and the Power of Creation

iUniverse books may be ordered through booksellers or by contacting:

iUniverse
1663 Liberty Drive
Bloomington, IN 47403
www.iuniverse.com
1-800-Authors (1-800-288-4677)

ISBN: 978-1-4502-8677-0 (sc)
ISBN: 978-1-4502-8678-7 (ebk)

Printed in the United States of America

iUniverse rev. date: 12/01/2011

CONTENTS

The greatest gifts that can be given to anyone are honesty and service. The following chapters of this book are a sharing of my personal journey through life, the gift of a service I wish to give the world. The words I have written come from the honesty of my own feelings and the observations of my own challenges and learning. They are recordings of things that have come and gone, and understandings that have entered me at times of great peace. Along the lines of honesty and service, I would like all the readers of this book to understand that what I share is a gift of words that I created to encourage others, and by no means is it meant to put me up on any pedal stool or make me any greater or less than any other being. It is important for us to all understand that we experience a gift from life to share our experiences with one another, and that is what I have chosen to do. With that, this experience which I write to you has two parts, a part which reflects upon a great lie, "The Lie," and a part which reflects upon truth. This book will begin with the part of my experience which I came to describe as "The Lie," and in honesty is something that still challenges me at times.

An Introduction to a Realization

I remember clearly the miserable feelings of my lowest points of depression. It was overbearing, the sorrow making me feel as if I was useless—and as if life were the most horrible punishment. Everything seemed so grim, and my thoughts and feelings were reflections of madness. It was as if I couldn't even move a foot without a shadow of insanity following me. I felt hopeless, as I did throughout many periods of my childhood, and as I had felt on and off throughout my life. Most would classify this type of depression, on and off, as bipolar disorder, and at one point I completely fit in with this category.

For a good part of my life, I faced pressure from surrounding circumstances, as is typical in human life. I was constantly surrounded by arguments, anxiety, sorrow, and aggression, while at the same time being pushed toward the infamous ideologies of success and achievement. I had myriad standards to meet, answering to various people and taking orders from every direction. I had built an analytical mind from everything, trying to break down every idea to please everyone, always trying to be someone else, somewhere else. I was caught up in every type of system, from various cliques to frequent different political views, always changing and always confused. Ironically, I questioned all these things. I questioned why people had such extreme ideologies, why people wanted me to be a certain way, why no one could seem to get along, and why I was such a prisoner to the negativity. At a young age, I knew this was insane. It made no sense to me that no one was happy and that everyone lived so vigorously by some definition, still not happy even when they supposedly fulfilled their selves.

Not only did I question the outside influences in life, but as a child, I also began to question myself. I would often wonder why I was on Earth, and toward adulthood, I began to question my feelings. As the insanity furthered, and I felt more and more hopeless, I really began to question why I was feeling so despondent. I finally hit a breaking point in life. I stopped everything I had been doing and opened my eyes to the insanity that was unfolding in and around me. For once in my life, I completely *recognized* the insanity—not just the insanity within me, but the insanity all over, which had been there since I came into this life. An introduction to a reality brought me face to face with myself and the world, and I had come to see that much of what *I* was allowing in me and thinking was a part of the insanity. A truth had begun to arise in me, a truth that much of what had been going on in my life seemed to be, and actually was, a lie. Even the feelings that pushed me into depression were being propelled by this lie. It was a shock at first to realize that for my entire life, I had been deluding myself through all the ideals, identities, and standards that I, and everyone else, had set for me. It was only after I could no longer take the misery in and around me that I came to see the madness.

Soon after this, I began to make my way into different spiritual teachings, and I eventually ended up in a martial arts class, where I picked up several different books that shed light on what had happened inside me. Ever since I have been on a personal philosophical, creative, and spiritual journey, and have come to understand a variety of wisdoms. From all of my understandings and experiences, I came into both a self and universal realization, a realization that what was driving me to my breaking point was also related to what was driving many others to their breaking point—and it was all because of what I came to refer to as "The Lie."

PART I

THE LIE

CHAPTER ONE:
THE LIE

THE LIE – THE FLEETING ILLUSION OF MY LIFE

The moment that I came to recognize the madness in my own life actually turned out to be a gateway to a higher understanding for me. Little did I realize that in doing so I was to stumble across one of the greatest dysfunctions, and as well a deep truth. The most shocking part of all of this was that I held, and always had held, that truth within me, even before I realized it. Even more shocking was the fact that no one could have ever *given* it to me, as I will not be able to *give* it to anyone else. I realized that truth in nature was far deeper than any definition, wording, thing or idea; it was beyond all mentality. That underlying truth is in a power that you direct, and every human being can direct, and it resides within the power of life itself. It is in the creativity that allows us to be here, the same creativity that flows through us and allows us to build, engineer, design, and manifest. Essentially, The Lie is the *idea* that something outside of us or that some mental construct or concept alone can give us true purpose or power. It is the dysfunction of our own thinking and mental state that take us away from the true power. This is exactly what I had stumbled across after I realized that the things occurring within and around me were insane. I had come to realize that being consumed by thoughts and ideas, along with anxiety from not living up to mentally set definitions, created my total misery. My deep fears and even some of my ideology unconsciously took me away from the very greatness I thought I was looking for. My depression *was* my mental fear and anxiety; these were the obstacles. I had come to see the fleeting illusion of my life, the illusion of whom I thought I was... an illusion perpetrated by fear.

THE LIE – BEYOND WORDS

I have spent much time in the last few years watching what has gone on inside of me mentally and spiritually. Along with self-observation, I have spent much time observing my surrounding environment, from my day-to-day human interaction, to the alone hours I spend outside or in nature. It is from these observations that I was able to recognize and feel where conflict and insanity began, at least within my own life. I was able to watch my own mental fears play out, and I was therefore able to go beyond my own mind in these instances. I am going to use some of these various personal experiences as a mirror for others to reflect upon so that they may come to be witnesses of their own experiences and become teachers unto themselves. What helps beyond all talk and walk is reflection; and that is what I intend a majority of this writing to be. For this book to assist you in being a teacher unto yourself, which you already are, and for you to understand any of what I have written, you must not only read, but reflect what is here upon yourself through witnessing and feeling it in your own life. This book itself is also a reflection and these words are arrows to the feeling and observation you must ultimately come to. In this sense, perceiving what is going on in and around you is the most fundamental step in *all* understanding. So with this, I have chosen to write about where I have observed most, if not all, conflict and insanity, which was rooted to my mental and emotional fear. As I came to recognize the fleeting illusion of my life, I was able to see that my own thoughts and fears created hell for me. I came to recognize that our fears are the underlying emotions and charges behind what I call The Lie; this is the best way to express how it works in words.

In relation to what caused my suffering, I described how the standards and definitions that I kept trying to meet and strive for brought me anxiety; this mind-set brought depression and anger. My own deep fears, thoughts, and beliefs had produced all of my unhappiness; they were all united in The Lie. Now, why would I relate my fears, thoughts, and beliefs to a lie? Well, the way I came to understand this was by watching nature and then reflecting it upon my mental state. I came to realize that there is no so-called clinical depression or insanity in the natural world—only humans seem to suffer from it. So if nature is not mentally unstable like humanity, then this is, in a sense, not true to nature. This is not to say that depression, or any other psychological disorder, is not real. These types of mental states are very real and can be quite compelling, but they are imbalanced and not at one with life; they have become a hindrance to progression and unity. In this aspect they are a lie. This is why I have come to call our emotional states and thoughts—the ones that bring us useless conflict, misery and discontentment—The Lie. There will be many descriptions of The Lie throughout this book, but **what occurs in *your* mind to imprison you and take you away from living and enjoying your life, as well as what separates you from the rest of life, is *The Lie*.** All of this starts within the very processes of the mind.

One of the most profound statements I have ever read points to all that is true and all that is false. That statement comes from the *New York Times* best seller *The Power of Now*, in which author Eckhart Tolle puts the title of the first chapter into plain words: "You are not your mind."[1] From that statement, I began to look at how the mind works, and I realized what really goes on inside it. An open door pulled me into understanding that my mind was a part of me, but there was a power beyond just my mentality. All the definitions and standards that I had lived by were created by me, *through* my mind. When this hit me, I saw that the workings of the mind, or thoughts, are just endless streams of information moving in and out of production; I realized that the insanity in my life was being produced via my mentality. Before I had even read his book, I had felt that something through me was bringing about madness; that something was ironically starting in my own head. When I finally snapped out of my own nightmare, I came to recognize that the origin of madness in my life arouse from thoughts and ideas.

The problem was really within what Eckhart Tolle described as identification with the mind, or identification with thoughts. We consider our thoughts, our concepts, definitions, ideas, and beliefs to be the supreme truth, attaching so strongly to our mentality that we actually become solely what we think. When we do that, we are no longer in charge of ourselves; our thoughts and definitions, the streams of information going through our minds, become the controlling power. The conflict within that is that there is more to us than ideas and thoughts, a matter of fact our ideas and thoughts are just possibilities; something deeper within us powers these. Metaphorically, all of our thinking is best described like a pond of possibilities; there can be so many outcomes for what we think we are and what we want to do. These possibilities are like fantasies, dreams, or illusions swimming around, and when we choose to, the power within us can bring any one of these out of the pond and into reality, or our ponds of ideas and thoughts can bring to reality hell for us. I finally understood that the hell in my life was born from an illusion; from a possibility—one that I had brought to life, or rather one that took me over.

Not every thought is that compelling, however. We only bring to life our most frequent thought-based illusions, or our most frequent thoughts bring to life what we think we are. Our thoughts are *just thoughts*, almost literally like computer codes moving through the program of a computer, and so the power within us allows and initiates the codes and information to move. That deeper power is the power of intention. Power of intention is one with the power of creation, or the power of life; *it is us*. In later chapters this will be the main focus, as we will see that the power of intention is behind all things. Intention directs anything to be. Prime example: if you *intend* to go to the store, you will go to the store regardless of the nine thousand thoughts running through your mind.

All of this may be a lot to fathom; however, the important things now, and at any point, are the processes of your mind and the processes that go on inside of you; *these are your reality*. It is important that we pay close attention to what flows through us; this is the variable for progress.

---

1   Eckhart Tolle, *The Power of Now* (Vancouver, BC: Namaste Publishing Inc, 1997), 11.

REALITY OF THE LIE

The self-realization I had experienced after I was pushed to the edges of depression led me to witness the force that was pushing me to insanity. It felt as if this force were significantly beyond me yet at the same time within me. This is because my own thinking and my own fears had taken me over. When mental processes run wild, when thoughts bring up situations and out-of-control ideas in your mind, you are taken over by them as if something outside of you entered your body and attacked you. Thoughts almost have their own life, and they really do. Thoughts can enter from any angle; they can arise from what you read, who you talk to, what you watch, and what you listen to. Someone else's thoughts in conversation, or even in music or writing, can easily become your thoughts. With everyone and everything you interact with there is an exchange or generation of ideas; there are thoughts constantly coming and going. Thoughts are the medium by which possibilities move, they are themselves possibilities, and they are the blueprints to action. Most importantly here is to understand that thoughts have a creative energy charge, a life force, and it is invisible. Thoughts can spark anything to be if enough energy is focused. If you are not aware of your thoughts, and what is going on around you, negative thoughts can enter, build up, and determine your moods. Thoughts can take over your life, and unoriginal ideas can rule your existence. Not surprisingly, thoughts, and even moods, transfer through communication and the "charge" of a thought or mood can easily replicate itself in your mind. When you talk to someone that is upset, you can easily become upset, and their ideology can easily become your ideology. However, we have power over this, just as we have power to power anything. Many of our ideologies do not originate within us, but we do generate our own moods and thoughts. Each individual person has individual fears and anxieties and this is a key example of how one's own self can generate madness. Our own individual experiences can lead to a personalized mood such as depression, or resentment, which may have started from something exterior, but none-the-less is within. Between outside experiences and ideas, to personalized thoughts and moods, misery can easily become your minds main production, and it can take over. That is what I felt when thinking to myself that I was not good enough, or that I needed to do this or that to be acceptable. This unoriginal and repetitive negative mentality took control of my life; it was like a wave of negative energy taking over my body.

On a metaphysical level, what I refer to as The Lie *is* a negative frequency, or force, that is derived from our own psychology. It is composed of the negative reactions, such as anger, depression or anxiety, from our thoughts, ideas, and mentality. Most of all it is rooted from the suffering and fear-based thoughts that have made us crazy, and we might consider it all the possible negative or evil things we have in our heads. Where else would all the madness in the world and any of our created conflicts have started if they had not arisen through thought in the first place? Thoughts through our intention have the power to direct our lives to be negative or positive; to be truthful, or false.

Quantum physics, the most recent studied of the sciences and mathematics, has even shown the direct relation to thoughts and energy frequencies, to help bring into perspective just how powerful our thinking can be. On a more mechanically visible level, psychologists use EEG scanners, and a variety of other devices, to measure the actual physical energy your brain goes through during your different states of mind. Some of these special types of devices can detect brain waves, and levels of your alertness are measured in those brainwave patterns. "Levels of consciousness in terms of levels of alertness or responsiveness are correlated with patterns of electrical activity of the brain (brain waves) recorded by an electroencephalograph. During wide-awake consciousness, the pattern of brain waves consists of rapid irregular waves of low amplitude or voltage."[2] How alert you are, and your state of mind, specifically if you are wide-awake, can be recorded electrically—enough said.

Regardless of which one of these views you look at it from, the activities going on within the brain and mind have a momentum and an energy that is not visible with the naked eye. In other words, what you think and how alert and not alert you are have a direct relation to the energy literally coming out of your brain and mind, and somewhere down the line, your thinking and mind can determine how your life is going to be. If you were to look up any research or documentaries on this, you would be able to find hundreds of studies and recordings related to how your state of mind affects you, and how it affects the world. But beyond the super science and energy aspect of it, it is imperative to know that The Lie, and all you can think of to be madness, starts within you. I know I am reiterating this, but it is a fundamental for transformation.

Before I got into the details and science of the mind, and the science of The Lie, I simply just felt and understood that something within me, within my own mind, was causing all my negative reactions. The prime example that led me to understand this was actually my own suffering. Going through the pain of my own suffering made me question its roots, and from there, I eventually realized that in my life, the psychological fear of me not meeting up to my expectations, and the expectations of others, was the force behind my anxiety and depression. I had come to recognize what was going on inside me. I also came to see that The Lie was not just this primary fear alone either, but various other psychological fears that played through my mind. From there, I felt it best to describe all the madness occurring in me as being rooted in psychological fear.

The best way to describe the force of The Lie, which took me away from actually living, *is* psychological fear. To me, there is no doubt that most of the world is wrapped in psychological fear—in some form of anxiety, paranoia, or worry—if it has not become blatantly obvious to you. Humanity has responded to these fears with insanity, through the various conflicts,

---

2   *Encyclopedia Britannica Online,* "**Consciousness**," http://www.britannica.com/EBchecked/topic/133274/
consciousness (accessed August 4, 2010).

dramas, and wars that we have instigated. We have spawned insanity from our psychological fears, from our anxiety and misunderstanding of each other, and ironically, that which is created from our fears can only produce more fear. This is seemingly the current state of the world: fear and war.

There is an even more significant reason behind why I call all of this The Lie, and that is because some of our mentality, excessive psychological fears, and the resulting insanity we have created from them currently serve no relevant or beneficial purpose in our existence. They have, in fact, separated us from living our lives and separated us from each other, just as a lie separates friends and family. The Lie is also created on the level of mind; it is created from the energy of our thoughts, which are charged from our creative power. In this sense, however, The Lie has no real power, unless, of course, we allow it to. This is because our psychology and thoughts are initiated by that deeper power: the power of intention and creativity, which is greater than mind alone. If we can focus on our thoughts or create and direct with our thoughts, then the power of intention to direct what we think and create is obviously greater. So the delusion that The Lie, our psychological fears, excessive ideologies, and insane thoughts, has power over us makes The Lie a lie.

CHAPTER TWO:
UNDERSTANDING THE LIE

THE LIE'S PSYCHOLOGY

To better understand the roots of The Lie, it is simply this: a fear created from mentality. It is a fear produced from, and programmed into, our thoughts. As well as that The Lie also consists of those negative thought patterns (anxiousness or worry), which turn into such cycles as phobia, aggression, depression, and so on. This is something I picked up both from psychology studies, and author Eckhart Tolle, and this type of fear and its reactions can all be re-termed as psychological fear. Psychological fear is itself biologically derived from natural fear. Natural fear would be the type of fear you would find in an animal when that animal is physically threatened and it runs. The animal has a natural biological reaction, or impulse, through its nervous system to get away when being threatened, and its body reacts in the same way you do when you are afraid. The difference is that animals do not have ideas of an event that has occurred. They generally cannot conceptualize fear; they primarily feel it.

Natural fear is integrated into our thinking patterns, and from that, it is psychological. This means that we can think about fear before we actually feel it, or we can feel it as we think it. Although psychological fear is derived from natural fear in order to help us survive and advance, it has mutated into a majority of thought processes and thoughts that have gone excessively beyond these purposes. This mutation of fear into our minds probably came about within the mind's ability to interpret things, and so at some point, we were able to mentally and verbally identify fear and anything that sparked the idea of it in our thoughts. Fear could be, and still is, charged directly into how we think. It would be reasonable to assume that as our thinking deepened, so did the complexity and power of our fears. Therefore, we even began to *think* fearfully, anticipating and judging situations and other people in defensiveness, including when unnecessary. Regardless of all psychological jargon, all that matters for change is the basic understanding of how it works and when it happens. You may even be able to notice a form of this fear based defensive mentality in your daily interaction, such as when someone you do not know looks at you and you think to yourself *"what is this person looking at."* This is an example of anticipated thought, which is itself psychological fear; it displays the psychological fear of not knowing, and the fear of threat. Defensiveness and anger are always underlined by fear; anger is itself a biological reaction for defensive purposes. In psychology this is called fight or flight, and it means that when a threat is occurring, fear kicks in to either produce a fight back with anger, or an escape is created for survival.

Today a significant amount of our thinking reflects this negativity and fear. It may be that with our survival state of mind, we have come to associate many truly non-threatening ideas and concepts as fears, and consequently have become more defensive. I have no argument either, that defensiveness is understandable, and it needs to occur in a world were threats are virtually unavoidable, but excessively defensive and anxiety based mentality have energized, or has at least helped energize, psychological fear to become mutant.

The most powerful and common psychological fear is that of the unknown, a fear of things that our minds cannot understand, such as life beyond physical death. Our human fear of the unknown has its purpose, and that is also for survival (as well as motivation for understanding) but in order to help you more vividly understand the dysfunctional aspect of this, deeply consider the presence of fear in any animal you have ever encountered, as exampled earlier. As mentioned an animal runs if its life is in danger, so you can say that it has a fear of the unknown or death, but that is more so a natural fear-based reaction from its body, and brief at that. When a threatening scenario is over for an animal (unless it is constantly repeated), the animal will usually resume whatever it was doing, continuing about its business as if nothing happened. That is because the fear it just encountered did not become deeply psychological, or charged into its psyche; minor emotions and situations (fear) do not become personalized to the animal. The animal also does not think about, consider, or analyze what would have happened after it had died; it does not fear a future or hypothetical unknown scenario. This would have no relevance to the animal or the animal's survival. This is again a psychological fear, a fear that goes beyond the scenario of a life-threatening situation and lives on in the mind long after the threat has passed. Psychological fear is useless to an animal because it would further distract the animal from realizing its liveliness and trap the animal in its mind, allowing a predator to easily subdue it. The only purpose for psychological fear and fear of something unknown in the human species is for ambition, preparation, and prevention of future conflicts and catastrophes. However, many psychological fears—specifically our fear of the unknown—have trapped us within our minds.

Psychologically, if we can trace back our fears of the unknown, they would probably lead up to some of the various superstitions, phobias, anxieties, and other evolved mental disorders that have plagued our world. What exactly do I mean by fear of the unknown though? It is as simple as this: fear of the unknown is fear of what you have not come to mentally label and understand. Some prime examples would be anxiety when meeting someone new, of course the fear of death, which is the ultimate physical unknown, and one that many if not everybody has experienced—fear of a future event that has not occurred. We tend to fear these types of things, or at least have feelings of fear when we think about them, because mentally we have not been able to identify or label these occurrences. When we do not understand something, our minds seem to register what we do not know as a potential threat because we cannot understand that thing's behavior or nature. When we do not know other people or are going to meet new people, we are hesitant to get to know them because we have not previously stored information on them. The fact is we have not been exposed to their personalities, and in our minds, something uncategorized or unknown can be that potential danger. Rationally, there will always be suspicion for one's own protection, but this mentality leads to anxiety. All of this comes down to fear of not having definition. This means that The Lie comes from our mental misunderstanding and misinterpretation of life; it is our attempt to give definition to life, to ourselves, and to others. Definition has valued purpose, but it seems as though our definition giving has taken us away from actually living, and it has even become destructive. On a personal level, though, fear of not having definition, and not knowing, becomes the psychological fear of not amounting to anything. Many people struggle to become and amount to some form of defined "greatness." This fear of not amounting to something was the very same fear that caused my depression.

This is also a part of the reason why we classify ourselves as many different things, and why we have created such strict standards for others and ourselves. At some point, we all want to know who we are and who everyone else is, and we want ourselves and everyone else to amount to something. In general, the human mind wants everything in life to amount to something, for all life to come to some mental pinnacle. This is why we have such various standardized systems and beliefs. That is what our minds and brains are generally set up to do: compute and account, interpret, label, and formulate. However, it is only through our understanding beyond the mind, through feeling and perceiving, that we can intuitively sense the purpose of life through deeper power. Some call that deeper power and intuitive sense spirit or consciousness, and that it also is.

Our definitions and standards, on the other hand, are just a system of comparison for us to communicate our individual realities with each other and are themselves predetermined thoughts and labels. Factually speaking, you cannot compare the reality of all of life to anything; there is no standard or single thought system to describe life: life is life. Reality is that life is endless, and all of life is comprised of the same universal elements and energy, so you cannot compare that everything-ness to everything or anything. We can understand how things work and break things down, but we can never definitively know anything, we can only express what something is. This is where our conflict arises—in the insanity we have created by attempting to make life something more through our fear of not having things defined, labeled, and amounting to something. We seem to be lost in the shallow aspect of life, stuck in comparing the physical and having our comparisons add up to some point for life to be, instead of letting life take its course. Standards serve their purpose, but to be lost in our ideas of comparison takes us away from life and the real purpose of life, which is beyond any thought or standard, and that is to live.

THE LIE, THE BIRTH OF THE LIE, AND STANDARDS

How did this all begin? When and where was The Lie born? Our psychological fears and our own mentalities are understandably the propelling force of The Lie, and these begin within our minds. This is the whereto of The Lie. The Lie is being born, or actually reborn and added to, every moment you are completely taken over mentally by psychological processes—specifically, the most possessive being psychological fear. Its actual birth date is of no relevance and will never be known because we cannot carbon date psychological fear or any of these possessive psychological processes. The only thing to understand about The Lie, then, is if it is taking you over—and that it is all within you. If we summarize the processes of The Lie, it is a combination of fear being charged into our minds, along with our responses to those fears, such as physical anxiety or emotional imbalance. It is a negative mental and emotional force or energy that imprisons you, and it once again starts in your head.

The key here is to understand *what is happening within you*. Always remember that everything is within you, and the so called way out is really the way in. A good example is watching yourself in a scenario you have not been in before. Notice the anticipation in your mind, for example, when you do something you have never done before, or when you go to a place where you have not met anyone. Almost immediately, you will have hundreds of ideas and concepts as to what is about to occur. When this happens, recognize what your mind is doing. In a new scenario, your mind has never defined or classified the experience, and so it is left unknown until you experience it. All the anticipation and ideas you are having are due to that underlying psychological fear of the unknown, and your mind will attempt to relate what you are about to experience to something previously experienced. Our minds tend to be very selfish, and they wish to know everything, it is no wonder why people can be classified as so. As soon as you see all of this, you have stepped ahead of the mind game. The mind game, which has become The Lie, is yet again to have everything standardized, classified, and defined, so everything amounts to something and equals some quantity. This is not to say that we should not define or have things labeled; this is just to show you what the mind does.

In our current world, the mind game is out of control, and I will not sugarcoat that. It can create much frustration, as I can attest to it. Our excessive living up to mentally created standards, definition giving and class labeling, and overproduction to accumulate the things we like, are all a part of the mind game that is causing hell on earth. The more we try to amount to something and have life defined, the bigger hole we are going to dig for ourselves.

To elaborate on standards, the literal definition of a standard is a system for comparison.[3] Now standards are extremely useful in communication, just as definition is. Being that we can compare and contrast things physically, standards are usable for expressing the quality of something—to help us realize what something physically is and how it can physically affect us. A good example of a standardized system that is extremely useful to us is the standardized system of food quality. We use standards to help compare and contrast what food is healthy and digestible for consumption, and what food is not healthy or consumable. If we did not have such standards, we would have a hard time expressing what to eat and what not to eat. On an even larger scale, we compare national food standards across the world, relating to which nations have higher illness rates based on their quality of food, distinguishing which systems work and which do not.

The main words to recognize here are "communication" and "quality." That is the purpose of standards, to *communicate* the *quality* of something through comparison; standards are not really related to quality itself. This is where it can be confusing: we can live so vigorously by standards, such as living up to a specific status or system, thinking that it will bring quality to our lives. The truth is that the standard has nothing to do with the quality of something. Quality is based on the creative nature of something, along with the state of what it is; the standard just helps you understand how it may feel or be to you. Quality in your life, then, is based on your comfort and contentment of life, on how you creatively feel. You can live up to the highest standards and be unhappy because the standard is just expressing the quality—you are the one interpreting and feeling the world.

A good example is this: suppose you struggle to have many cars and homes. Those cars and homes may be of high quality; however, you may be extremely miserable trying to get them paid off, and will probably have a higher psychological fear of losing them, so the quality of contentment and comfort in your life is not there. If you have the means to acquire what interests you, and enjoy every step in the means of acquiring, then that is a different story. The difference is in if you are attempting to gain something for the sake of meeting up to the standard; if you are forcing yourself to go through hell to have many cars and homes because it makes you a "better" person. You are depressingly lost in the standard. Standards are here to let you know how something may physically affect you. Your actual living self and inner state does not need a standard. This is not to say that you should completely ignore standards and disregard them, for they play a part in physical well being. Through higher standards, we can see what makes us physically feel better, and that is significant. However, the moment standards mentally take us over and we seek truth and freedom from them is the moment we become prisoner to our fears and thoughts of not meeting up to standards. This is The Lie at work. The whole concept of a standard has taken you over, when it was just a tool and a thought in the beginning, a concept

---

3   Webster's Dictionary and Thesaurus, "**Standard**," 1999.

we made up. Once again, this is the reality of The Lie—concepts, thoughts, and ideas being mistaken as the whole of life, as the creating force. We have become lost in our own creations and in the processes of our minds, taking psychological fear, our ideas, thoughts, standards, definitions, and concepts to be the only purpose of life. We have forgotten that we can power all these things or have power over them.

WHY IS DEFINITION A PROBLEM?

Now, you may be asking, and it came across my mind, why having definition is such a problem. You may even be asking yourself, *Isn't definition what makes me unique or special—does that not make me, me?* The answer to that is no. Definition, like a standard, is only a way of expression and understanding through words; it is trying to clarify something. Through definition, you can never know anything—you can only express or clarify the characteristics of something. In fact, the definition of definition is literally to give clarity;[4] nowhere have I read that definition means to know. The only thing that you can truly know is what you are, which is life and the power of creation. Everything else is subjected to change, including the personalities of yourself and others, emotions, environment, and the materials that encompass you. Life itself is the fact; everything else is a product of that fact.

This is not to say that definition and expression are not important, that they serve no purpose, because they also do. Our abilities to express and define things allow us to help understand each other. They help us to progress, develop, create, and engineer. Definition is a way to share with each other our abilities and creative powers, and that is why we have developed communication and definition. However, we have lost ourselves in definitions, losing sight of the creative power that powered them, the power that we have, which *is* our uniqueness. Definition may be able to express or give clarity to what or who you are, but those words and expressions are not what make you unique. What makes you unique is not what you can be defined by, or clarified by, whether it is money, status, personality, beliefs, relationships, and so forth. What does make you unique is your creative self, the freedom to do as you choose, or your spirit as it has been called by many. Definition has become bondage, bondage from what we "think" we are—the ideas, wants, personalities, relationships, and so on. I mean, if we were all truly free and unique, would it matter how much money or how many things we all had? If the entire world were all truly free, the ideas and identities that humans have for one another would completely no longer matter. However, we can be free, through creative power and understanding.

Truthfully, the freedom to do and the freedom to create are what make you unique, for out of these freedoms, you have endless inventive possibilities. However, when you are bound by a definition, by the wants, status, and all the other forms of definition, you will find it impossible to do as you please and create as you please without something from your "definition" tugging at

---

4   Webster's Dictionary and Thesaurus, "**Define**,"1999.

you to do things a certain way. You may have to be in some group and be part of some definition to progress, or follow certain methods in life, but if that is only what you see yourself as, if that is "who you are," and you cannot have any periods of creativity or feel freedom at all within yourself, then definition has become your personal bondage. If we look at what definition has become for humanity, a false sense of life and an attempt to escape psychological fear, then there can be no dispute that definition has become a catalyst for our conflicts, and that is a problem in itself. If people cannot live without being defined by something, without fulfilling their desire to achieve a certain status or needing some idea to have meaning to their lives, then I can surely say that the problem of definition and The Lie are more than just evident; they are catastrophic and characteristically demonic.

THE LIE – YOUR PERSONAL DEMON

I have come to view The Lie as demonic. To me, The Lie is no different from a demonic entity. If we look at what so-called demons usually do, they spawn fear and possess, creating insanity, chaos, and, ultimately, suffering. The Lie *is* a demon. In fact, for every human possessed by it, The Lie is a personal mental demon; we have built our own personal hell from it. Some of the definitions and ideologies that we have taken on are like the stories in which our mental demons whisper into our ears in order to begin taking us over ... and eventually possess us. The thinking chaos (the excessive defining, greed, desire, drama, status, etc.) within our minds becomes strong enough to completely take us away from the reality of planet Earth, and that is our enslavement. Sometimes these thoughts can feel like they have external power, and they do when negative thoughts and emotions can enter during the absence of realization. The mind has much power, and when ideas like greed and lust enter the mind they can become demonic and spawn irrational behavior and feeling. I recall an instance in my life where I was with an ex-girlfriend and my feelings and desire took me over to the point where I felt no control over my body, I literally felt possessed. Not only did I feel like I had no control, but I felt sick as it was happening. Inside of me there was a heaviness I cannot completely explain, and I truly felt a negative presence shadowing me. After the incident was done I realized what had happened inside of me, an emotion and an idea (a desire) literally took possession of me. Ever since, I have taken what I felt that day as a symbolic lesson from the universe; I had directly felt the negative power that can come through one's own mind. Bottom line: from my lack of total realization this type of feeling was allowed to occur, and *we* allow exterior thoughts, negativity, demons, and/or whatever other term there is for that which can be considered mind controlling, to possess us when we are not watching. Just looking at it from psychology alone, it is clear that thinking and the mind can have a supernatural grip over us, *especially* if emotions, memory, and thoughts in some can lead to the committing of violence and crime. If the mind is powerful enough to build civilizations, then the idea of hell in the mind can also be as powerful as a civilization. Regardless of what I feel at times, it is within my own self that I must face hell and insanity; my own mind is where my personal reality starts. It will be up to you to also face what happens within you, regardless of what you feel or believe.

Many different spiritual teachings and religions speak of demons and possessing entities, and this is no surprise to me. Demons in terms of thought processes are the haunting and possession by emotions, ideas, and mental definitions that take you away from the moment you are in. All the psychotic behavior and violence in the world, including the maximum extremes, are reflections of those rampant mental thoughts, ideas, and emotions. When negative emotions and thoughts take over, they can lead to negative and evil actions. The root of all evil is in the mind, *if* we allow the mind to grow evil.

Who are we, then? As I have read and heard from various spiritual teachers, all that matters is to know who we are not. We are not the ideas and definitions we have created, we are not the thoughts and concepts in our heads, we are not the psychological fears, desires, and emotions that seem to run us at times, and we are not anything we can verbally understand. Therefore, that leaves us with only one understanding: within us is the power that allows all of these to be, a power that cannot be compared to anything. This is, in essence, what I sum up as the power of creation—and is the very reason I have titled this book *The Lie and the Power of Creation*. Later on I will get deeper into this power, but it is time that we discuss facing what happens within. This is awakening, and the first step to awakening is facing the disturbing factors. In that, awakening means you must face and witness your own psychology and, specifically, psychological fear.

CHAPTER THREE:
AWAKENING TO THE LIE

AWAKENING TO THE LIE – FACING PSYCHOLOGICAL FEAR

When I came to see The Lie, I saw how fictional it was. I did not understand The Lie until I was on the edge of the cliff of depression, ready to jump off, and there was a main reason for this. I had come to recognize it when I had no choice but to *see* and *face* my psychological fears. Instead of looking for a way out of my pain, I was forced to look directly at the source of my pain. It was inside me; it was in my psychology. That is when I awoke; I came face-to-face with my own demon. The only way to be able to transcend the insanity, misery, and fear in life is to face them—your own psychology and your own fears. Transcendence occurs when you recognize what goes on inside of you.

There is no running from yourself and even the psychology of others, just pure realization; that is the means for change. Everything that can emotionally affect you is powered from *your* thoughts or enters *your* mind, and by running from your thoughts and psychology, or looking to blame outside of this, you will only end up playing a game with yourself. The moment you realize that fear is in you or that an emotion is driving you mad, acceptance (the way in) is the only way out.[5] When you realize and accept whatever is happening, what you are feeling, and what is evident, that *is* true realization, and a step out of the mind game has occurred. Acceptance, or what many teachers of Zen call non-resistance, has become a practice taught by many recent spiritual teachers, and is age old wisdom dating thousands of years back. Granted this is easier said than done, I have tried acceptance, and it works. By facing your situations and accepting what is happening, you allow for the reality of transience to come into you, meaning

---

5   Eckhart Tolle, *The Power of Now* (Vancouver, BC: Namaste Publishing Inc, 1997), 35.

that what happens is only temporary and fleeting compared to the span of all existence. Deeper than that, acceptance implies that you are no longer controlled by a definition or standard; you are not mentally consumed by an ideology or the idea that you have to be something else, or somewhere else, other than what and where you are. Yes, you may have or want a special title or goal, and may have to do things to survive, as we all do, but the fact is there is nowhere to be other than where you are momentarily, and nothing greater than the power in you. At some points you may need to make changes to stages in your life, but the power is within you and your intention, not any of your actions alone. Back on the note of mind games, not accepting what you are feeling and what is happening is self-conflict; it is the minds attempt to be somewhere else, someone else, and feeling something else. Nobody, or rather no one's mind, wants to accept non-pleasure filled emotion and no mind wants to be definition-less, or without the "highest" or "specialist" name, status, or standard. Why should it, your mind is designed to survive in the easiest way possible and it is programmed to achieve and gain. Your mind may not be able to completely accept being definition-less, or accept the losses and pain in life, but you can. If you can go deep enough into what you feel, that is if you can go into your fear, pain, discontentment, anger, or resistance, you may be able to see for a moment beyond yourself, and glimpse the antics of your mind. You may actually be able to see that what you maybe cannot accept is a part of your mind's programming or conditioning, and a part of your mind's own fear. Facing your undesired emotions means that you realize they have to die at some point. If you realize any of this, then you realize that there is something more to you than just the thoughts, emotions and ideas that can consume you. That something more is power.

Your mind itself is a product of that power—the creative force, or energy, if you prefer, that makes the living, awakened, intelligent you. That power is fearlessness. The best way to achieve this understanding is to just witness. Even if you have intense emotions and thoughts, let them play out. Thoughts and emotions will pass no matter how intense, especially if you just watch them happen and become a witness instead of a prisoner. Eventually, and hopefully, that reality of transience sets in. Thoughts and emotions are never absolute; they are relative to scenarios and subject to change. Maybe that reality will trigger the understanding that the fears and emotions going through your mind are also just products of your mind, and they only have an effect on you if you forget that there is more to you; if you forget that you are a conscious power. This may be the essence of what was said by Franklin D. Roosevelt: "We have nothing to fear but fear itself." It is a great statement about psychological fear because why be afraid of what is fabricated within the mind? After all, the mind is where this all starts, so you should be observing what is coming into your mind. This puts you above all of your psychological fears and negative emotions. In any scenario all you can do at first is recognize what is occurring, and so the initial step you should take in any scenario is witness everything playing out, within you and outside of you. The next section says it all: you should simply be the witness of the insanity, not a participant.

WITNESSING THE INSANITY

Before anyone can come to understand something, he or she must first observe or bear witness to it. As I discussed earlier, I came to understand The Lie by witnessing the insanity in the world and the insanity within myself. Without that moment of being a witness, without observing the insanity and recognizing it being there, awakening to The Lie might have never happened for me. There is more to being a witness, however, than just looking; it means that you are completely aware, that you are in a state of *pure* realization. Anyone can say that the world is insane or that what he or she is feeling is crazy, but it takes a larger step to actually *realize* and *watch* it happen within. If you are realizing the insanity, then you are seeing how *your* own thoughts and mental processes are helping to create and continue madness.

The moment I recognized that my *own* psychological fears were driving me mad was the moment I came to *pure* realization. I stopped looking to blame other people and realized that all of this was occurring within me, even if it came from outside of me. This is facing the facts and it is the one giant step, in Neil Armstrong's words, that we all must take in order to become true to ourselves.

The best way to be a witness is to watch the various components of The Lie at work. We should look at its different angels and see how they flow through our thoughts and reflect in our emotions. Witnessing all the different angles and aspects of what can happen inside of you leads to pure realization. From the time I have spent watching my own thoughts and emotions I have been able to witness the various components of The Lie. Even now, The Lie can still consume me if I am not in a state of realization or if my mind is so adrift that I am not there to witness its processes. Watching the different angels and components of The Lie at work is a major part of pure realization, even after you may have initially realized. The first thing to look at carefully, however, is what you *want*, because wanting is generally definition seeking. In this sense, what you want, or what you think you want, is more than likely the main component of The Lie at work.

THE LIE'S MAIN COMPONENT: WANTING

I have come to see that The Lie's main component is wanting, for what can better give "definition" than that which is gained through wanting, such as material items, personal status, attention, and so on. Enjoying something that you obtain or receive is not the issue; the conflict resides within the psychology of the wanting behind whatever is obtained. Consumed by The Lie, we have come to want things insanely, just to fulfill our mental idea and definition of having something. Many of us could probably care less about having whatever it is that we feel we want.

It is the mentality of gaining that possesses us. This is the main component of The Lie, where our thoughts are focused on wanting to gain for the reason of mental definition.

Even deeper is the fact that psychological fear perpetrates our seemingly never-ending wanting. I discovered that in the past, I had wanted things compulsively in order to have more than others around me, and I wanted to be "better" than they were, and this was a part of my own psychological fear of not amounting to something. Fear was motivating me to want. In my mind, I thought that by having more, by gaining more, I would be better and more fulfilled. Of course, later I discovered this was a lie. I truly didn't care for the things that I gained. They were only a way to make me feel as if I was something more. The things that I did gain were only there to distract me from my discontented reality. For brief periods, having more things made me feel like more, but that was soon toppled by the fact that I had to struggle more in order to keep my gains secured. Not surprisingly, many things that I put in extra work hours for ended up in pawnshops or, even worse, in the garbage.

I am not saying not to have things either, but what I will stick to here is that we are being eaten alive by our own psychology of wanting. We think that by obtaining more, by continually getting new things, that we will be happy and defined. We may even think that the things we get will make us feel better or occupy our time, and they will at first, but in the end they are just things. The insanity is in the compulsion to have. That compulsion is almost an addiction, and in some cases, it is. It can become an addiction in which you think that the more things you acquire, the more you will amount to something. That fix of having may make you feel as if you are something, or that your time with whatever you have is worthwhile, but that only lasts so long. The more you have, the more you will struggle to have more. Some people become hoarders for this reason. They become so imprisoned by their mentality of "having" as their purpose that they keep every little thing they come in contact with. Truthfully, you can buy and have things to enjoy, but if it becomes the mind game in which you must always have and keep getting more to be content, or have bigger and better things to keep you defined and your mind at ease, then you are a prisoner to The Lie, and definably an addict. If you were to compare this to drug addiction it is no different, as time progresses, more and more drugs are needed to satisfy the abuser, and the same can be with how people desire and want things along with status; as time progresses, more and more things and status are needed for "contentment" to satisfy the seeker. Wanting, along with our definition seeking and desire to amount to something, are those mind games that keep The Lie alive.

The fear of not having, not becoming, not adding up, and not making it are all the same dilemma as well; as we already know, they are mind games. The moment we obtain something, whether it is a thing or a label, we are defined by what we have obtained, and our minds process a "gain." More than likely, we are not even conscious of this or what we are even doing. We just want things because they appeal to us. Psychologically, that appeal is still there as a part of definition seeking: what I have come to recognize as the adaptation and gaining process. This is to say that over time, we mentally become adapted to certain customs and objects, and these become a part of our likes, a part of what appeal to us. The things that we like, those things that appeal to us, become programmed into our minds as a part of who we are; our definition. Our psychology becomes: *I like this; it appeals to me; it states who I am; and I should have this.* Obtaining what appeals to us is not a problem. The issue at hand is that we can become so lost in what appeals to us, so lost in the idea of *"I like this because it is me,"* that we become solely what we think of as "me." Our appeals and the concept of this is "me" are also *just ideas;* they cannot compare to the reality of power within you, and are subject to mentality. Just remember that being consumed by appeal, style, genre, or definition can cover up the true uniqueness and freedom you have within.

Once again, all this originates within the processes of the mind, so even what you like or what appeals to you is projected from the same place where The Lie projects itself. The Lie keeps us thirsty for definition, for things that make us "us," and then we must gain in order to be who we are. It is that very psychology of *gain* that causes us disturbance. It is as if there is an office in our minds where accountants and lawyers are checking and securing everything, adding the numbers for everything in life, making sure we have all the gains for the quarter. This is what keeps the office of our mental definition going. We all want to be somebody or get somewhere—at least until we discover that "somebody" and "somewhere" are just things we made up. It seems as though some people are in a rush to get to that "somewhere," as if they are in a race to get to the truly nowhere "somewhere" we created. This is exactly why wanting is a component and product of The Lie. It breaks down to fear-based psychology. *"If I do not get to this point or I do not obtain this, no one will accept me. I will be useless and purposeless; I will not be happy."* That general mental process occurs when we are in the heat of trying to get something or somewhere. The truth here is that through fear, you want things, but without fear, you can just have things, and let them come and go, without going through hell to get them.

Through The Lie, humanity is subjected to wanting things destructively, meaning people begin to seek possessions, personalities, and material constructs all at the cost of understanding and living true life. The Lie enslaves millions into believing that things and desires will bring about happiness and freedom through definition and that is the biggest fantasy story in the world. Millions are enslaved to themselves, just as I was. For years, I believed that I needed things to make me happy, and when I obtained those things, I just wanted more things. I would go to a job not because I enjoyed it, but because I needed the money to buy more things that I didn't really need. It was the same thing with school. I would go to college classes not because I wanted to, but because I was told that I should get a degree to obtain a higher-paying career. I was always in a hurry to get out of my classes because they were requirements for a certain degree that I truly did not want. I was living my life to feed The Lie, to give myself definition, and consequently, I continued building the insanity within myself. Shockingly, I was also living out The Lie for others around me, including family. I needed to do this or that to be accepted, to be held to the specific standard of being "me," and I would suffer in trying to live up to how others had defined me. The Lie in others had developed an image of who I was in their minds, and it was up to me to fulfill that image so they could process me as "one of their own." This contributed to the lie-based mental idea of who I was, so I felt that in order to be "me," I must do certain things, have certain things, and become certain things. The wanting from within me and from others took over my life. True happiness and relations were subsequently almost blocked at that point. In general, relationships between people become blocked when wanting becomes the purpose of connection between individuals. It should be no wonder why relationships have become so dysfunctional; they have become a part of the illusory composition of The Lie.

WANTING TO AMOUNT TO SOMETHING: PSYCHOLOGICAL INSANITY IN THE HUMAN RELATIONSHIP

The Lie can warp every aspect of our being and living, and it most certainly has, even to the extent of the relationships we have with one another. This is easily demonstrated by the increasing divorce rates, increased domestic violence and familial conflicts, as well as the increasing violence occurring amongst youths in the education system across the United States. This should be no surprise either, as the relationships humans have with one another have become part of the composition of The Lie as well as a reflection of it. Because of out-of-control psychology, the concept of a relationship with someone has perverted and prevented a true link between people, becoming a structure for The Lie's existence. People may relate to each other, and often do, for the psychological fulfillment of amounting to something. As our own psychology is seemingly programmed to attempt to know everything and have everything defined, the human relationship has become a part of this definition seeking.

Although there are relationships in which people truly want to be around each other for that sake alone, day-to-day interactions and relations between people are still too often based upon the sickened psychology of relating to others based on definitions and status, what others can do for them, and how people define who they are. People will be friendly and reach out to another because that person can have an influence on their income or personal recognition. When a superficial relationship is made, for a temporary period, someone's psychology has amounted to what it was seeking, and another definition has been created. *"I now know this person; I can get to this point by knowing this person,"* is what we sometimes think, and we've all done so. What is fundamentally wrong about this is that the point we are trying to reach is impossible because it is a point created by our psychology, and it leads to discontentment and disagreement. Having things amount to something is a process of the mind, an attempt to calculate everything, which is impossible. Not surprisingly, when people do not gain what they want from a relationship, there is argument and conflict. The real conflict is that we base our relationships on this knowing and amounting standard, just like our wanting of certain objects. This is an example of almost the exact mental process: *I know Jim. Jim is my friend. Jim would do this for me, and Jim would never do that to me.* The funny part of this is that what Jim would and would not do is part of the criterion or standard for Jim being a friend, and that knowing Jim is through this criterion. So Jim is a friend if and only if Jim does this but does not do that. So in this case we only know Jim through the creation of what Jim is in our mental preference.

The whole idea of a relationship has become an almost mathematical process of the mind, using the formal reasoning of "if and only if" to sum up a connection. Even sicker is that we use that criterion for our family members as well. Many families give love to a specific member and disregard others based on their standards and criterion for what a family member should be. *I love you if and only if you do what everyone else in the family does* is what seems to be the equation for what it means to be loved by some families. *"I brought you into this world, and I can take you out"* is one of my favorites. Having a child is like having a commodity for some; whenever someone wants, they can just throw him or her to the side. It seems as if some people would spend more time with their children if, when they were born, they wore a label stating, *"When I grow up, I will be a lawyer or businessman."* This is just a reflection of how extremely sick relationships can get between people, but the reality is that the relationships humans share with one another have become perverted in this form of thought process. We have all done it: compared and contrasted friends, put people into categories, and even neglected certain family members based on what they did or did not do for us. That is The Lie.

GROUPS, CONDITIONING, AND THE CULTURAL LIE: THE GLOBAL HUMAN RELATIONSHIP

Beside personal relationships between individuals, The Lie has also warped the relationships groups of people have with each other. This once again relates back to the definition and labeling process of our psychology. Humans relate to each other based on their cultural and group identities, which are the definitions and standards they have taken on from others around them. This is something I paid keen attention to when I took sociology. All humans have some form of group or cultural identity. This is not to say that being in groups or in a culture is a problem, because it is not. However, our own psychological processes disrupt and distort the beauty of culture and our social interactions. Our minds work on conditioning, and the more we are around something or around a certain idea, the more that idea has a chance to possess who we think we are. This is where The Lie perverts how we relate to each other. We can become so mentally conditioned to groups or cliques that every idea and standard of a particular group or clique can take over our lives; we can become exactly the label or stereotype of a group rather than a member. When this happens, we no longer enjoy the connectedness of the group we are in because the standard of the group has become the focus. Instead of wanting to be in a group just to be around others or to share with others, some people remain in groups because they have become defined or excessively conditioned. Conditioning applies to all things in life, and the more repetitive a condition is, the more possessive it can be. I have found a very good way to detach from the possessiveness of my surroundings, group mentality, and conditioning, and I call it "*space your conditionings*." In recent years, moving around, meeting and communing with new people, and even taking breaks between different activities (and at times some were habits), have been a way for me to create space between my conditioning. Giving breaks in between weeks and days for whatever I was doing and whoever I was around lessened the compulsion of those activities, and not to mention it helped to break habits. In this, the ideas and emotions of whatever I was doing and whoever I was around had less momentum over me, and I became less attached to ideologies and feelings. It may be good to stick with certain ideologies, but the more possessive they become, the less unique and helpful they are. Just as it is with the human relationship we are discussing here, once ideology and mental conditioning take over, their purpose of helpfulness and enjoyment can easily diminish.

As is typically discussed in, and a major aspect studied in, any sociology class, the reason we first formed groups and developed cultures (along with cultural conditioning) was so that we could help each other and share resources. The first societies in the world began from tribes, which were traveling groups that helped each other gather resources and food. Eventually, tribes became larger and developed into societies, and then larger groups of people began to trade and share with each other. Groups and societies formed for our beneficial survival, developing so humans could help each other live easier and more artistic lives. Societies then began to develop the arts and entertainment, as well as different styles of living, and these became what we call the culture of a society. Culture was an artistic expression of a group's way of life, but eventually The Lie came in and people became lost in the definitions that their minds affixed to the culture.

In a more modern sense, we have become so attached to the ideas of what is current and popular in our culture that we forget that our culture is here for us to enjoy and help us relate to each other. We can take on the style of our particular culture or group and forget that it is an artwork for us to embrace; we forget that it was designed out of creativity. We developed cultures, groups, and even the styles within our own families so we could share with each other our uniqueness. I love to surround myself with the creative and artistic manifestations of all groups and cultures; however, in the aspect of The Lie, cultures and cliques have become the next most destructive thing aside from a moon-sized asteroid hurtling toward Earth. Total attachment with a group or culture blocks true understanding and detracts from the beauty each culture and social group has to offer us. Oftentimes, as it is presently, it causes groups and cultures to steer themselves toward conflict.

There are even extreme groups that base their entire purpose of life in defense of their definition. They believe that their groups' particular styles or ways of life are "right" in their extremist approach. Many base their extremist beliefs on their history and their mentally preset believed justification of "right." This is happening in the world today: clashing cultures and social systems all backed by a sense of "our standards" and the idea of whose style, culture, and system of life is "right" and whose is "wrong." The cultural lie is one of the most dangerous forms of The Lie, breaking way for regional and global conflict. Extremist group mentality allows for the persistence of The Lie, continued through definition defense. The Lie can possess the masses, putting them into a thought cycle of dominance. Some people will inherently throw themselves to death to feed The Lie with the ideology of "this is right." Wanting and personal definitions, combined with the collective definitions of The Lie, are the equation for total sociological and global disaster. Presently, the actual structures of our societies are a product of The Lie, and this is consequently mentally and physically unhealthy. It is just as the infamous spiritual teacher Jiddu Krishnamurti once stated: "It is no measure of health to be well adjusted to a profoundly sick society." The Lie has become a strong negative energy and is polluting entire groups.

"A PROFOUNDLY SICK SOCIETY"

Jiddu Krishnamurti was right on the dot with the idea that it is ill to be well adjusted to the sickened relationships humanity has developed amongst its groups. We can just look at the wars and imbalance we have created in the world from our fears, identities, and definitions of each other, and there is no argument that it is sickening, not to mention insanely destructive. We can simply look at the design of society and how it has manifested itself in the world and see that there is a major imbalance, creating conflict. One of the greatest examples I can use here is the abuse by society at large in terms of gaining wants. Just as individuals will create hell to get something, so will groups. A significant amount of our global society is prized on the idea of the continued feeding of wants and "righteousness," and in that, The Lie is able to possess people to do whatever they can in order to feed the incessant wanting and ideologies that controls them. Wars are fought, and countless millions are killed, burdened, and suffering, all originating from some form of selfishness. The reality is that better living has nothing to do with material production or specific ways; it has to do with mental and physical well-being, based on freedom from within, creativity, and natural balance. Imbalance in our lives and in nature has become the cause of illness in the world, not the lack of anything material or ideological. Society through The Lie has become the imbalance. Humanity continues to perpetrate war, and creates weapons capable of global destruction, all in the name of something. The examples are all around, and there can be no denial of what is, and what is evident is that The Lie has put the world in turmoil. This is not a blame game either. We cannot blame a specific society or group; The Lie can play itself out through almost any person, and the only way to transcend it is to face it individually. The same lie that is causing all the wars in the world and all the problems in your society is the same lie that is playing through your mind. It is all connected; you charge

The Lie in your own mind, eventually spreading your thoughts and emotions to others. Life is a collective energy, if you choose to look at it like that. If you see that you are one of the channels in that energy field, then you will understand that just by coming to realize that The Lie is here, you are making progress in the world; you are changing your energy in that link. When you change, and your perception changes, so does the world within you, along with some of the world around you. There may be madness all around, but the freedom within your ability to realize is greater. That realization brings you into understanding that you do inevitably have a choice, a choice *not* to be possessed by mental ideas, by likes and dislikes, wants, definitions and any other ideologies or thoughts.

Chapter Four:
Continuity of The Lie

Not only have we helped to create The Lie, but we continue it through our polluted mental concepts and creations. Humans have given themselves definitions and stories, becoming possessed by ideas and identifying with The Lie, and, in turn, have become possessed. From that possession, many humans conceptualize and create through The Lie. Many of the things humanity has conceived have been considerably negative to the advancement of life. Just look at how the weapons and some of what we watch and hear have almost been designed to separate and categorize us. It is imperative to understand how we have created, how we are creating now, and how we are going to create. That "how" is answered through our memories, through what we have stored in our minds and reflected upon. Our memory of events and experiences has allowed us to retrieve past information to be usable for current situations, for current progression. However, the memories that we use to advance have also become a means for which The Lie's creation is continued. In this sense, understanding memory, especially in yourself, is a way to understand if memory is helping you or corrupting you.

Memory: Friend or Foe?

Memory served and will always serve a major purpose in human existence, and that is because knowledge arises through memory. Knowledge is the accumulated, stored, and understood results of past experiences. Through memory, knowledge allows us to prepare for future scenarios based on the results of past situations. So the intention of knowledge is understanding, and in that is memory's significance. Memory is here to help us understand what has worked for humanity and what will not work for humanity. It is a learning tool, and through learning is understanding. Memory, therefore, only serves this purpose: it is an assistant in helping us figure out what we need to do now, and how we are to continue progressing.

However, there is a downfall to memory, which is that a majority of memory in humans actually serves no knowledgeable or reasonable purpose; it is simply an excess accumulation of experiences with no relevance to current situations or conflicts, and this is because of The Lie. In fact, through The Lie, memory is creating more conflicts than it is helping us solve. We can surely see this in action in our day-to-day lives and in the conversations we have with each other. I seldom hear others refer to the past for a solution; many conversations I hear from others about their pasts are complaints and dislikes. I have even noticed this in myself, and I can catch it arising at times. In complaining and disliking, in regret, there is no solution for whatever issue is occurring in the moment; and oftentimes, there is not even an issue to begin with, until past experiences are brought up. So humanity is defeating the purpose of memory by ignoring the results of previous experiences, along with reliving past experiences and regretting them, rather than seeing what will work or what will not work.

It is clear what works and what doesn't, and our present world is not putting this into action. The greatest examples I can give for this are social instability and social conflicts. We know that continually changing laws, regulations, systems, and sometimes even standards does not solve any social problems or instability. It creates future instability, yet groups continue to create more rules, change laws and regulations, and emplace new systems to stabilize a society or a group that is failing. But the question is how you can force stability on something that is unstable. You can't exert force on a wobbly table, expecting it to balance out—all it will do is tilt—yet humans continue to believe that enforcing new guidelines and harder ideologies will create stable societies. The foundation must be fixed at the bottom, where the imbalance is occurring, where people and nations need to be unified, where civil engineering and technological advancement should be priority. But we are not learning from past experiences, and The Lie through humanity continues to create further instability, with humans repeating the same processes and fights that have been going on since the beginning of civilization. When will we look at the past and finally fulfill the purpose of memory by saying, "This just doesn't work"? I used memory here as a collective example. The truth is that all humans should be using memory to progress their own existence. We should figure out that certain things that we have done individually in the past are a hindrance to us, and we should look to the past and see what benefited us throughout our existence. If a certain pursuit in school is not interesting to you, why should you continue to pursue it? If a certain group of peers makes you uncomfortable, why should you continue to commune with those peers? The fact is that most people become entwined in their experiences through The Lie, thereby creating a story for themselves and giving themselves definition. If we manifested memory for its purpose, we would no longer repeat the same mistakes, and we would instead be knowledgeable, comfortable, and progressive in our decision making. Experiencing and experience teach us, or at least they should be teaching us, but if we continue to allow The Lie to live through our memories, we will not learn anything and will continue to be miserable.

CONTINUITY OF THE LIE OR FINALE?

Human invention comes from that creative aspect of our minds. Inventiveness has led way to tools, technology, and the building of civilization. However, over the centuries, *we* have allowed the spread of fear. From atomic and biological warfare, to our violent forms of communication, The Lie has made a name for itself through the spread of such intimidation. It is not too far out there to say that this insanity has physically manifested itself through the mind of humanity. It's amazing how The Lie has turned the power of our minds into becoming miserable and destructive; it has turned the power of our creation, and life, into hell. However, all it takes is to see the truth, the truth that The Lie is here, and that we have power, to begin to dissolve it. Once we realize that we help power The Lie, we can stop powering it and take back our power. Then the door to the truth opens—the truth that we actually are the power, the power to do anything and make anything consciously. The truth will then shine through, and we can restore ourselves as the creators rather than the possessed…we can send The Lie to its finale.

PART II

TRUTH

CHAPTER FIVE:
WE ARE THE TRUTH; WE ARE CREATION

THE TRUTH IN YOU

The human world has become subject to psychological fear and to the resulting insanity of our own mental constructs, which includes all our anxieties, wants, likes, dislikes, beliefs, definitions, and so on. It may seem like a grim world, as if fear is the predominant state, and that insanity has turned into a social norm. However, all of this is illusory compared to the truth that propels all life, a truth that resides in all creation. You are that truth. You, every human being, and every life form are as well that truth. I have come to see the truth everywhere in this universe—in every tree, animal, person, star, galaxy, and in every creation—for the truth is life itself. It *is* creation. The truth cannot be defined; we cannot clarify it because the truth, being creation, is endless.

It took some dramatic occurrences in my life to understand this, but when I came to it, it was like no other understanding I have ever had. No one was forcing me to see this, and better yet, no definition or standard was propelling my understanding. I simply came to realize that in every religion, every book, every philosophy, and every idea that I had come across, there was the power of truth, because all of those ideas, concepts, and beliefs were, and had to be, manifested through one power, the power of creation. It is that power of creation or creativity, the raw potential for things to be developed, thought of, and shared, that is the foundation to all existence. With that I also realized that there is no standard, definition, or identity to this divinity; *it is limitless*. This understanding helped me let go of my obsession with mentally defining life, at my attempt at giving identity to the power that needs none. Ironically it was often times that pursuit to know everything, to define, that took me directly away from this true greatness.

Through the actions of our creative nature, it has become evident to me that we are here through this power of creation, for ourselves to continue that very same power. It has nothing to do with "knowing," but rather understanding and becoming one with that creative potential. I have gone through many philosophies, many definitions, and many ideologies, but the truth all breaks down to one, the power of one: the power of creation. I have come to accept all beliefs, philosophies, and ideologies as truthful in their approach, and as a part of the evolving of humankind, for eventually these all lead to the one common understanding: everything here is and was created, creation itself is power, and life is all the art of that creativity.

The power of creation is a whole truth, and we may realize various different truths within our lifetimes; however, it is our own power of creation and the power of creation itself that have allowed us to express, interpret, understand, and choose what we deem to be true. So we may all have different ideas and concepts as to what is true, but these are all *created* within ourselves, and ultimately we have the power to do whatever we choose, especially when we break free from our own mental demon, The Lie. Our power to create is beyond that of this physical world—this ability is truly what makes us stand out. Creation is the purpose of life, and every human harnesses the power of creation, so therefore every human contains the truth within him or her, regardless of how the person is defined, classified, standardized, or systemized. You have the power to do and create anything, including the ability to either continue The Lie, or the power to dissolve it through the realization that it is all within you. We are the creators, and we have become possessed by mental creations. Is it not time that we realize that the power within us, the power of creation, is the true power, not whatever thoughts or ideas are running though us? The power of creation itself is beyond all forms of life, both physical and mental, which are products of it. We are all this power and we derive it from that total power of the universe.

Consider another famous quote from Jiddu Krishnamurti: "We are the world." Access this, and you access the truth. Realize this, and you will realize The Lie is just a fabrication and has no true power over you; you are one with the real power. Reality is that your identities, definitions, status, wants, beliefs—and even how you look and dress—are just forms, ideas, and concepts, and they have no comparison to the power that is within you. When you see that the power of creation is inside you, you will step to the level of creation itself. You will merge with creation; you will become the truth.

CREATION

Everything in this universe is clearly a product of creation, whether we understand completely how things were created or whether we created them. The definition of creation actually means to bring something into existence, and so creation is literally everything.[6] This is understandable, even though ideologically we have made it difficult to understand. We must see that creation is every aspect of life as well as all the elements of life, and all these are created forms. It includes all the geological bodies and biological organisms. It includes every human and every animal; all of us, and this entire world, obviously, were brought about in some creative process.

Science has helped us understand how intricate creation gets, and it has helped us see how unique and interconnected it is. All the elements that make up our planet break down into microscopic cells and atoms, and they all have reproductive creative processes. Humans and animals can give birth and reproduce; cells split and multiply to make up tissues and organisms; and atoms add or discharge subatomic particles to create elements. It is as if every atom, cell, element, and organism is set up to continue to create or bring about life, and that is truly the case. Even all the invisible atoms that make us up are products of energy that we cannot see, and that energy is always fueling us and bringing about life. There seems to be an intention behind all of it, and that intention is for life to exist. The intention behind creation is literally, then, its definition, the intention for things to be brought into existence. This is complex yet simple, but that is the universe: a paradox of simplicity that is complex.

The simple complexity is that everything is the same with the same reproductive nature, yet so intricately different for the purpose of individuality. Every aspect of life is set up with the intention or power to produce a continued diversified version of itself; life. Why else would invisible energies and atoms formulate complex molecules and elements that make up countless physical forms? They must have the intention or design to do so. This is why energy forms different subatomic particles, which form atoms, which form elements, and these, in turn, form every bit of matter and life in the universe. The intention to create, or the intention of creation, we can call the force of creation. We may not be able to explain completely why this is, but it is evident. Life is here because of that intention: the intention to create—or rather, the intention of creation.

THE INTENTION OF CREATION

All we can do is understand creation for what it is: the intention for existence. This is all that needs to be understood when it comes to creation: creation is intended, and humans also posses the intention of creation—they are products of this power. This is why we have such unique, creative, and powerful minds; we can direct our intention to create what we want through our minds. I like to describe it on the deepest level as creation creating though us. There can also be no dispute that you do not contain within yourself intention and creative power. Look at any aspect of your life, specifically how you communicate. Your words are spoken from your intention to speak; they are created. See that you *are* the intention of creation when you speak,

6   Dictionary.Com, "**Creation**" (1), http://dictionary.reference.com/browse/abyss, (accessed 12/6/2010)

write, or communicate. When you execute any action or intend to do anything, you are using your creative and intention-based power. Even if you choose to stand on your head, the intention to do so has created the motion and form in which your body moves; the intention of creation has been used to formulate the position of your body.

All this comes to the fact that we are the power of the universe, and The Lie sets us astray from this understanding. Truthfully, The Lie was also a product of the intention of creation, and being based from natural fear, its intention was to help us survive. Once again, though, The Lie has outlived its purpose and is now separating the human species from true power. We are becoming lost in the forms of creation, from the definitions and ideas in our minds, forgetting that the power of creation and intention are in us. The time has come for us to understand this power, and that we can use it to transform any energy, even the madness within. The Lie can now serve its final purpose in our evolution: it can be transformed into something else, and it can be transformed back into creativity.

Many people have done this in the past. Various extremely creative and insightful individuals have transformed the energy that was within them, the energy that at some point was possibly The Lie, into creative expression and inventions. If we look at individuals such as Mozart, Da Vinci, Galileo, and Newton, we can see that they used their energy and their intention to create in the greatest ways possible: by constantly manifesting and engineering sciences, arts, and technologies that advanced the entire human race. Now is the time to transform this energy in order to progress our creative existence, and that is what we are here for, to use our intention of creation to transform. With this, we can see just how powerful we are and evolve through transforming The Lie and transforming ourselves.

FORMATION AND TRANSFORMATION OF ENERGY

Creation is composed of energy. This has become a universal understanding with the evolution of science and mathematics, and we can clearly see that all matter is a product of broken-down atomic energy. We can also see that energy is a transferable and transformable source. It can never be produced or destroyed, as Isaac Newton stated, but only put into formation, reshaped, reformed, or transformed. When you eat, the food becomes energy, when you turn on a light, energy is being converted from some source to make that electricity, and so energy is the material of creation, and it is constantly being transformed. Just as we learned in science class, atoms and elements change to make different forms and states; the energy that makes them up is always changing. This reformulation of energy, the transformation of energy, is the reality of creation. Always transforming energy, atoms, and elements continue the cycle of life. The relevance of this to humanity is important because humans also have the power of transformation through our creative intention. We are created in the image of creation, in order to create.

Understanding this, we can now look at the universe and see that energy, or life force, is in constant motion—or rather, it is in constant transformation. Energy is itself thought to be by some scientists as the constant, and it is constantly changing forms. This must be understood not just in nature, not just in how things change physically, but also in how humans are also meant to change and transform mentally. The intention of creation intends for us to transform our own energy in order to continue the process of creation. The transformation of our own physical and mental energy is what allows us to progress. Our form, whether physical or mental, is not permanent; it is always changing because the universe is always changing. This is the nature of the universe, the transition and transformation of forms, all underlined by the one source of intention that powers it. This is another way of looking at evolution. Evolution is just creation in its natural state, transformation, and rebirth, and so everything evolves on some level in order to bring about new formulation. This is why humanity has jumped the barrier on the level of mental energy; we have evolved in the process of creation in order for the intention of creation to continue us on the path of its intention (we are creation's creation to create). Humans are a transformable form as well as transformers of form.

HUMANITY'S RESULT OF POWER

Everything that has ever occurred in the history of the human species is a direct result of the intended formation and transformation of energy, which the human species has harnessed through the mind. In simpler terms, humans created all the sociological and psychological environments that are currently here. We energized everything to be what it is, and through our intention of creation, it was brought into existence. To look at this on a directly physical level, if there were never the intention of creation for the automobile, if we never intended to invent the automobile, we would still be riding horses. The same goes for any other technology ever brought into existence; the intention of creation allowed us, through our thoughts, to bring all these concepts and inventions into this world. We helped form and transform energy into these types of creations. However, this power goes on an even deeper level, as we have already discussed, on a level of our own psychology and feeling, and we have helped to bring into this world psychological insanity through the same power of formation and transformation.

THE TRUTH IN THE LIE

All the conflict within the world, and within ourselves, can be related to our ability to form and transform energy through our power of creation and intention. This is the truth in The Lie: that The Lie is just a product of the true power that is in us, and that The Lie itself is only a form. On a personal level, all the drama and problems within us are just formations of energy, which is our psychological energy. We can charge how we feel based on how we think, and the opposite is also the case. We have gone over how thoughts and emotions have a "charge" to them, and our emotions and feelings can themselves be transformed or recharged. It may sound easier than it is to do, but all that is necessary for change is this understanding: you allow for whatever emotion to enter you and charge yourself in any way from there. If something negative enters you, it may be charged negative, but if you do not react to it, or let it takes its course without becoming absorbed, you do not allow for it to further charge you and balance is allowed to occur. You may even use that power to create something, such as a poem or song, during a period in which you are feeling seemingly bad, and in doing so, you are using that power to transform and balance out. We are the power to bring about peace and tranquility, enjoyment and truth. Creation powers everything, and it can make anything powerful, even how we feel. However, as we evolve with this power, we will come to see exactly how significant it really is, and through the process of transformation, we will begin to build a truer world.

CHAPTER SIX:
THE *POWER* OF CREATION

THE HUMAN POWER OF CREATION: A TRUER WORLD, A TRUER YOU

Through our understanding of the power of creation, we can finally come to see *how* we can use it to change our lives on a personal level, resulting in a truer world. There is no argument that you and every other human can create and will continue to create in some way, shape, or form. You are a contributor to the process of brining things into existence, in whatever aspect that so happens to be, and you are here as a part of the human power of creation. There are actually many different aspects to our ability of creation, and in every action you commit, there is the propelling force of creation and transformation. However, we must remember that the true purpose to everything in the universe is creation itself, which is the bringing of existence, the bringing of what I call the art of life. Our intention to bring something into existence, or our intention of creation, is what aligns us with the divinity of the universe. When we separate from each other and creativity, or forget that we are a part of everything else and a part of the entire creation process, then we separate from the purpose of life and truth.

THE HUMAN POWER OF CREATION

The power of creation itself is channeled through our minds, through our thoughts and conceptual processes. On this level, the power of creation can be directed into many forms of action. The human mind is designed for the processes of learning, understanding, communicating, labeling, inventing, and engineering, all processes for continued creation, so the human mind is a device for creating. This is where the human power of creation comes into play. With enough focus and intention, we actually tap into the total power of creation itself, and from there, it is a matter of how we transfer, or formulate, this power.

THE HUMAN POWER OF CREATION IN THOUGHT AND CONCEPTUALITY

The mind can be best understood as the channel for the power of creation; it is where our power of creation is centered. The mind is an uncharted part of us; we cannot see it and it consists of thoughts and endless ideas. So when we talk about thinking, and about our minds, our minds are just the endless streams of information and concepts going through our heads, as mentioned in the beginning chapters of this book. Thoughts are the energy flow of creativity, and they move like a stream. If you have ever been caught up thinking for hours on end, then you may understand this. During the hours you were thinking, the thoughts continued streaming through your mind until you became aware of them. That is because you left the flow uninterrupted, and a frequency will continue until it is interrupted. To sum this up, thought *is* the constant frequencies of creative energy moving through the mind, and this composition of thought makes up the mind. This is also what I meant by earlier stating that thoughts were the medium for possibilities; possible creations move through your mind every second in the form of invisible mental energy (thoughts). So, in reality, what you are thinking is just a constant flow of mental energy, and you can direct it. This is where the human power of creation begins, within our intended or directed thoughts and conceptual processes, and from there, anything can become.

However, most people do not realize that our intention is what propels our thoughts and conceptuality. The Lie has taken the place of many people's conscious intentions, and so The Lie (greed, anger, fear, past ideas, etc.) has instead become the intention that dictates the thoughts and creative processes of the unaware. In other words, The Lie is creating thoughts and formulations instead of people doing so consciously. There must always be the force of intention behind something for that something to be, and either we direct that intention or The Lie will. Once there is an understanding of this, then thoughts and concepts can be directed freely and creatively, without the bondage of our own negative state of psychology. Look at it this way: once you realize you can direct your thoughts and concepts from your power of intention, then you can begin to create and think as you choose, but you must first see that The Lie is there; you must see that a past idea, definition, emotion, or ideology can be creating and thinking for you. The truth is that we are all either a product of, or the director of, creating intention, and it is up to us to choose which we end up being. Eventually, we are all supposed to direct our intentions consciously; in this, we evolve to the process of the universe and become the guardians and channels for power.

The best way to begin using the power of your intention is to focus your intention little by little on a specific creative aspect. If you begin to focus your thoughts on something specific in terms of creating, you will begin to see just how powerful your intention can become. A good example of this is anything spoken or written. Communication is the most common aspect of our power of creation because every day, we are speaking or writing or both, and through our intention, we bring into existence the words we speak, write, and communicate. The more you focus on what or how you are saying or writing something, the more you will understand how to allow that creativity to flow naturally, and how to direct it into what you choose through the power of intention. Observing and directing what you say, write, and communicate is one of the best ways to come to understand and practice your intention. This is why talking to others and writing in a journal are exercises in therapy and relaxation. They are both processes in which you are directing your mental energy and the power of creation within you into becoming the expression of words rather than a buildup of negativity in your body.

THE HUMAN POWER OF CREATION IN COMMUNICATION AND WORD

Many do not realize the true creativity within our communication process and the words that we speak. In fact, one of the most fundamental creative aspects of our existence was, and still is, the way we communicate. If we did not use our power of creation to create communication and words, we would not have advanced as far in intelligence as we have, and we would have had a more difficult time surviving. It is our ability to communicate that has allowed us to express better ways of survival, and it has allowed us to teach each other everything that we have come to understand. Words themselves are a power, produced from the power of creation that flows through our thoughts. In this aspect, we power words just as we power thoughts: from our intentions. Our intentions of creation allow words to be brought into existence, and we can intend our words to be whatever we wish them to be. We create words to mean what they mean; we make them become what we want them to be. This is why words only have significance through intention. Words that we categorize as happy are intended to describe happiness, so through our intention to describe the feeling of happiness, we developed an expression, a word, called happiness. However, the word happiness means nothing without the intention to express behind it; it is just a sound. If you say you are happy in a negative tone, it is noticeable that you are not happy, and now the word happy, which you have given identity to, no longer describes what it was intended to. Your expression of happiness is contradictory; it is a lie. We can take a word that means something else and change it into another expression easily, even though it may be confusing. A good example of that is sarcasm. Once again, the intention behind the word is what really informs you of its meaning.

Because words are a product of our intention, through our thoughts, words also carry different frequencies of mental or emotional energy based on our intention; words can be

The Lie. If the intention of a word is derogatory or meant to cause hurt, it will carry negative energy and may be received as an insult or threatening. The negativity of a word can be felt in its intended frequency. Insults and any other intentional hurtful words are The Lie, and they are only used when The Lie has control over a person. If you look at The Lie and out-of-control psychology as negative energy once again, then it is easy to see that negative energy will only attempt to bring about more negative energy; demons can only summon more demons. So when someone insults or uses intentionally hurtful words, the intention within that individual has become to continue the negative energy of The Lie, and The Lie has control over that person's intention; an idea is fighting an idea.

Of course, this is unrecognizable during a dispute or argument because those who are in an argument and exchanging negative energy do not have focus on their intentions, and so The Lie takes over their intention to create and speak. Negativity then becomes the intended creation. In this sense, the intention of creation creates no matter what, whether an individual is aware or not. Negativity from The Lie travels through the words of others and will continue as that uninterrupted frequency until that energy is transformed at some point. If you have ever been in a busy restaurant or other form of fast-paced business, you will surely notice this. All it takes is one individual to become upset and speak through The Lie to put everyone in a bad mood. This is because the negativity will travel through all the individuals of that business and be transferred through words and expressions. The negative energy will continue on its frequency to many people, and it can easily travel outside its origination point. This is why when some individuals have bad days at work, they often cause their loved ones at home to be in a bad mood as well; the negative energy is continuing its frequency, literally changing the energy of others to match its own. It will continue until someone becomes aware or consciously chooses to balance out the energy frequency by creating and offering positive words or expressions to others.

Our thoughts and words are themselves actions, and thought, word, and action are synonymous in the process of creation. Relevant to us, our intentions will always result in some form of action, whether it is mental in thought, communicable in word, or physically put into existence. Action in the power of creation *is* the constant transformation of energy. This results in the physical formation and transformation of energy in physical action. Both thoughts and words are a part of physical action.

THE POWER OF CREATION: ACTION

Creation, or anything in the creation process, can be considered action. Action exists on every level of energy and on every level of life. By definition, action is anything done or performed[7], and on every level of life and energy, there is frequently something being done or performed. On the level of electricity, energy is constantly being converted into various voltages and strengths,

---

7   Dictionary.Com, "**Action**" (2), http://dictionary.reference.com/browse/abyss, (accessed 12/6/2010)

and conversion of electric energy to other forms such as chemical, light, and heat are always in performance. So on just this one level of energy, action is being committed constantly.

More relevant to us is action on the physical and mental level. Action on the mental level is performed in thought or in state of mind. Action on the physical level occurs from our sensations, including sight, touch, smell, hearing, and tasting. The action of our thought processes and of our minds is connected to our physical abilities. So the action occurring in our minds is linked to action we commit with our bodies, and even the action in our minds can have physical results. Physical action is therefore the result of action on multiple levels, and what we think is a part of the actions we commit on a daily basis, even though we do not visibly see our thoughts. So when we think, there is action, and what comes through our minds is creation, having the potential for physical existence. Therefore, our power of intention and creation allows us to do as the universe does, and we can commit a multitude of actions to physically alter the surrounding world and ourselves. This means that we can change how we think, feel, create, and physically exist, all through the same power that propels all states of matter and existence. Even when we just think, it brings about emotions that we can feel; they are physical. So, in some way, action will lead to a physical reality. It is just a matter of the intended result of that action. If people are consumed by thoughts that make them feel insane or helpless, their physical actions and feelings will represent that helplessness and insanity. However, we can use this to bring about continued beauty within our own creations.

There are many ways we can become empowered by creation through our direct physical actions. Some of the examples of using our directly physical actions, instead of being consumed by our thoughts, can include creative hobbies such as drawing, writing, building, singing, and physical fitness. These actions are all physically committed or tangible. You can put your thoughts into direct physical work, or action, instead of them putting you to work. Hobbies are a great example of this, for you find what you like to creatively do without any attachment to definition and thought. The universe came about into existence not from a definition or classification, but from that free creativity and the physical action of that creativity.

THE TRANSFORMATION OF ENERGY THROUGH PHYSICAL ACTION

By understanding the power that there is in action, and the physical actions we commit, we can use our physical actions as a way back to the power of creation. Now, of course, it is possible to do this all mentally alone, without a single directly physical action, but it would require nonstop observation and patience, which is not generally an option if you have a multitude of tasks to complete daily.

Due to the momentum of The Lie, of the psychological fear and insanity in this world, it is often too difficult to just jump and grab control over the intention of your thought processes without minimal awareness or training. This is the essence of Eastern philosophy, what is called mind over matter, and generally Eastern religions and schools of art practice patience and observation over the intention of the mind. It takes much effort to completely awaken to every thought process and fear, and to be a witness to them all the time. Gradual awakening starts by being a witness and then generally drifts in and out of observing, into direct physical action.

One of the most common ways to begin to reconnect with the power of creation and to transform the energy within you, then, is through the physical realm, through physical communication and physical exertion. Even Eastern religions and schools of art use physical action as a means of reestablishing a connection with deeper power. This is why many monks in Eastern temples, such as in Tibet or Thailand, spend hours in physical workouts and hours in disciplines and teachings by masters. Physical action is not just in physical movement, but in mind, as I am stressing again. Many empowered individuals, including monks and martial arts masters, do not just train physically or mentally alone, but both with physical drills, creative exercises, reading, and philosophical teachings. Remember that thought, action, and word are synonymous. What you think has physical affects, what you speak you can physically hear and think about, and any action you commit from there is physical, so all three of these are one. This is why it is good to have a variety of hobbies or physically exertive outlets, so that way you are able to help convert and direct the different energies and processes within you, including what goes on within your mind.

This brings us back to The Lie, our own creation of psychological fear, insanity, and suffering, and the reality that these are themselves energies, which we are resisting converting. By not realizing that we can physically and mentally convert the negative energy within ourselves, whether it is anger, fear, or just outright psychological pain, we allow them to build. These negative energies alone must have some physically active result, the result of physical suffering.

In recent years, psychologists have shown that various mental disorders and anxieties have lead to physical problems within the body, and there is no doubt that this is a reality. The negative energy, which we build mentally, and the psychological fears and insanity are converted into physical problems, such as heart disease, high blood pressure, and various other physical disorders. There are many different physical actions that you can commit through your intention which will allow the negative energy within you to be converted into creation. Using the powers and natural intention of the universe to transform, create, and/or physically commit action is the tool to your own liberation from the psychological fear and insanity that we have all energized.

CHAPTER SEVEN:
THE ASPECTS OF PHYSICAL ACTION

The world is guaranteed to physically change, and so are you. However, the way or type of change is deemed through the intention behind physical action, and the planet itself will endure change from physical action based on the intentions of nature. In this sense, we have the ability, no different from nature, to direct our physical actions and initiate change. There are three main aspects in which humans can direct physical action resulting in physical changes. Physical exertion is the first aspect of physical action that we will discuss. Next is physical interpretation, which allows us to physically communicate and share understanding with each other. Finally, there is physical creation, the ability for humanity to physically design, invent, engineer, and build. These three aspects are what our power comes down to, and we can sense and perceive the resulting transformation of energy from these aspects.

PHYSICAL EXERTION

Physical exertion is what we think of the most when we think of physical action. It is what you can consider to be direct physical movement and exercise, and is the way in which your physical body exerts energy and transforms itself. By getting up and walking around the block, you are committing physical exertion as the energy of your body, in that simple process, is focused on the act of movement and the perceptions you experience during the walk. By walking, running, exercising, dancing, and even moving around at a job, you are allowing the body to release stored energy into whatever physical movement you are doing, and therefore converting energy. Even through such things as breathing and blood circulation the body is transforming energy which is required to power those vital processes. Your body is constantly renewing itself in some form of physical exertion and bodily movement, and that is why all physicians stress the importance of exercise—you are helping to give rebirth to the cells and structures of your body.

Relating to The Lie, the greatest part of physical exertion is that you are also taking the focus of your energy away from your mental and psychological excess, and putting it into the action of something physical. Even just taking that walk helps you transform negative energy because you are focusing the energy into that physical act. This is why people are told to take a walk or take a deep breath when they get in disputes. Doing so takes the focus of the energy off the negativity charged, redirecting it into the walk rather than the physical act of a fight. Somehow, the human body is going to convert or release built energy, whether or not an individual consciously chooses to be involved, and that is why some people frequently get physical when angry. In physical aggression excess built energy or negativity is released; the human body must let go of that which it accumulates, including emotions like anger. At this point it should also be no wonder why diseases and physical problems occur in some people; the body and physical being of an individual react to the madness being released from the mind and insanity in or around them. Even the mind seems to not be able to handle its own chaos at times, and it is almost as if the body's reaction to the stress and anxiety creates issues or physical problems to signal change. As a young adult I suffered from severe stress and depression, and as a result of my anxiety I developed acne problems. The stress in my body was causing acne, which I realize now was there to tell me the severity of what was going on inside me. As I steered toward peace and began to transform, the acne faded. When things become excessive there are physical results which are there to signal change or bring about renewal. So this brings us back to the intention of all energy, which is designed for transformation—it *is* rebirth. If there is a lack of physical exertion, no self-renewal, and no mental transformation within a person, then the energies within them will begin to destroy the body, and even the psyche, in an attempt to bring about the needed change. Energy is always in motion and always converting, so we have options: flow with the energy process and be consciously involved in the transformation of your physical energy and mind, or go against it and let the energy convert into something that will speed up the destruction of you. Just by walking around the block, or being involved in the movement of something creative, you are helping your body do what it does best: converting energy and renewing itself, not to mention putting focus on the life of your physical being.

PHYSICAL INTERPRETATION

The second most common way in which we are converting energy, and the most influential in terms of our mental state, is through our ability to interpret our existence physically. In a simpler sense, this is how we understand and project our lives. Now thought, word, and communication are a product of our intention; they display and help us use our power, and these abilities allow us to interpret the world physically. Some common examples of physical interpretation are lecturing and reading, for we receive information and teach each other in these ways. Listening to a lecture and using your eyes to read are both processes of physical sensation, allowing you to take in information. Energy is also required for us to think about our existence as well as communicate facts, ideas, concepts, and beliefs to each other. Thought itself is an action, and the way we interpret our physical lives is through thought, which, consequently, is the action of our mental energy. By thinking, we are using or transforming mental energy in order to sense and understand something. How we interpret life and how we take in information is how we transform the energy of our lives. Our physical interpretation of life, the information going in and out of us, can literally be considered our programming, and we are programming it. This programming is conditioning; the very same conditioning that was discussed in the third chapter.

In the personal or psychological outlook, conditioning is the storage and interpretation of an event from the senses which leads to thinking, analyzing and acting in scenarios. To use a basic example, if you touch something you have never seen before and it hurts, you will sense the pain from what your brain interprets, and then you can think to yourself, *Wow, that hurts. I'm not going to touch that again.* It usually takes only one time for you to realize not to touch an object that inflicts severe pain. Obviously, much of conditioning occurs through repetition, in which your mind stores the memory of something after it has been replayed so many times. An example of this is how many times your parents or guardians told you to do something when you were growing up—and how many so-called bad memories you retained from not cooperating. Eventually, either you figured out to do what they said to avoid the consequences, or you became cunning and figured a way around the scenario. You became conditioned to what you were supposed to do, or you conditioned a new way for yourself. Your mind stored whatever seemed to work out in the most desirable way.

Conditioning is not a bad or a good thing; it is just the way we adapt to our environment. It allows us to physically understand and get through this world. However, we can control how we condition one another and ourselves—and how we interpret our lives. I have already given one example relating to this, and I described it earlier as "spacing your conditioning." However, the main focus is to realize that we are *beyond* just conditioning, and that most of our conditioning, besides our biological reactions, is ideologically passed down. People become negative, aggressive, or anxiety filled because mentally they are conditioned to think that way. Throughout our lives, we can unconsciously store in our memories that a certain behavior will get us our way, or that being aggressive or sorrowful is the best way to survive and live. The mind can program that if we get what we want from a specific behavior or ideology, including those that are chaotic, that the specific behavior or mind set is the correct way.

Our mental energy, our thoughts and our memories, are there to help us store information and continue creating and surviving. Therefore, what we put into our minds—and what we view, hear, and sense—affects how we think and how we exchange information with each other. This is physical interpretation, and if we look at history—specifically, if we look at The Lie—we can see that the energy of many of our interpretations of life have remained negative and untransformed. This can be illustrated by the countless wars and genocides we have committed on each other; the ridiculous amount of suffering that has seemed to walk hand in hand with us throughout every era of our history.

This brings us to the process of physical interpretation, which is literally your ingestion of information. The old saying "Garbage in, garbage out" is such a true statement. The information that we learn, the things that we sense, end up categorized in our minds. When we read something that provides us with information, we store that information as knowledge, and that can affect how we choose to view the world. The more negative information we ingest, the more negative things we are likely to feel. The more positive and freely or creatively we view things, the more creative and positive we are likely to feel. What we have physically interpreted in our past more than likely has become how we are interpreting our present. This has been an endless cycle, primarily because most do not even consider this process. We continue to perceive and sense violence and pain, even inadvertently, and it is consequently affecting how we interpret life today.

USING PHYSICAL INTERPRETATION FOR TRANSFORMATION

At some point or another, we have all fallen victim to some emotional drama or to a scenario that we perceived as bad. We have all experienced the feelings of fear and anger, and now it is time to see the processes of those interpretations, their significance, and how we can use them as transformational tools. We can use this aspect of our power to transcend some of the hell we have created. If you have realized any of this, you may start to become aware of how you have been interpreting the world. You may even begin to realize that how you look at life may be through the eyes of past interpretations and definitions. This is the point from which you can act when necessary, instead of reacting from past ideas and thoughts, which is what happens most of the time.

There is a major difference between action and reaction. Most of how we interpret the world, and even some of what we do, is reaction; it is repetitive from past ideas and years of conditioning. We perceive the world through emotions and ideals that were here before we were born. Humanity has been interpreting the world through the reaction of what it has been conditioned to, and seldom do individuals act out of unconditioned interpretation.

Not many people take true action. They may be acting, doing, or thinking something, but it is generally a reaction to something predetermined. Many of us, including myself at times, react from ideas that have no relevance to what is occurring now. When we truly choose to act—to choose to commit an action or intentionally think—there is a direct awareness of what is occurring in and around us, and there is no past idea or desire involved. When you commit true action in a scenario, your prejudgments will not chain you down.

It may sound difficult to be almost completely mind free, not to have a judgment about a scenario you are involved with, but try it just to see how it feels to be in a conversation or read something without taking a side on what you are mentally ingesting. In this sense, when you are listening, you are truly committing the action of listening, or when you are reading, you are truly committing the action of reading, versus having a predetermined idea of what you are interpreting. Instead of thinking, *Wow, what this person is saying is not making sense* or *I like what this person has to say*, focus on the energy of the conversation and focus on what is trying to be expressed, rather than thinking about what you like or dislike. When you do this, you step to the point where you can witness what is being said, rather than become consumed by it through what you think. For example, even in a conversation that is seemingly negative, be observant, and attempt to understand what is happening: negativity is channeling itself through the conversation of another. The Lie (someone else's predetermined ideology or negativity) is manifesting itself through the words coming at you. When you cease to have your own ideologies determine what is being said, or when you cease to take offense to something, you can come to see how words or ideas can interpret for you your reality; they can change you if you let them. In this you come to realize the power of interpretation and that you are the one who can do the interpreting. In summary, you are aware of interpretation, and therefore free from its possession. You may even start to become aware that a significant amount of the conversations and interactions people have with each other tend to include the reactions of prejudices already stored within the mind. Many times, there may be conversations where you notice more head nodding to things agreed or disagreed on by you or another—rather than true listening. This is important to be aware of, as it can make a world of difference in your relationships with others and how you learn. It comes down to this: either you are in conscious control of what is going through your head and what you are doing or listening to, or The Lie and all your past ideas, emotions, or definitions are doing the talking and walking.

The main focus in using your interpretations for empowerment and creative living is that as long as you realize that you are the one interpreting your life, the less effect past interpretations will have on your perception. Instead of being bound to one form of information or type of knowledge, you can act, perhaps choosing a book that can teach you something new. Maybe you can even listen to a new type of music without judging it right away.

When we learn, we should also be observers of how we are interpreting the information. We tend to sit in a classroom and react to what information is coming at us; we opine and offer our input. Instead, we should allow the information to come at us and not immediately like or dislike it. It is just like when you are having a conversation; you may have opinions or emotions as to what is being said, but be aware that these are probably your own past interpretations. Then some of the information coming at you may not be judged or labeled; you may actually be able to realize more, or even come up with new ideas of your own based on what you have just heard.

Allowing information to come at you without interpreting it from your past, or some definition already played out in your mind, can actually help you problem solve because you leave room for new concepts about a subject to arise. When your past interpretations have stopped blocking the entire communication between you and another, there is a stronger link for learning and experiencing. There will be less of an argument and more responses such as "Wow, I didn't realize that" or "That is interesting." You can just listen and learn without letting your emotions get in the way, which ultimately refreshes your understanding of life. From our understanding of our power of interpretation, we can go into our final aspect of physical action, which is physical creation. What we physically create is a reflection of what we interpret and have interpreted. It is the past "new" information stored in us that has allowed us to progressively build the world. What we learn from, we advance on and consequently create from.

Physical Creation

Physical Creation is the most unique form of physical action. Being the result of both physical exertion and physical interpretation, it consequently requires both to produce results. When we physically create, we bring new forms into this world beyond us; we give birth from our energy to whatever it is we are creating. Whether we are creating a piece of art, music, a craft, a project, or even a conversation, we are using physical action to the maximum in putting the power of creation into play. This seemingly simple idea of being creative is one of the closest ways we can get to being truly "who" we are. We are all comprised of that creative universal energy, and that energy is intended to create, when we flow with it, and when we are creative, we become who we are; the universe. So when we are the universe, we create with the intention to create. We do it out of joy, really, just because. Putting this to action is genuine power. This is probably the best way you can relieve yourself of stress as well—taking all that stored energy and making something of it.

You will find it hard not to focus on a creative act that you enjoy; it gives you a sense of liveliness, like childhood. Children have that free creativity naturally because they have not yet fully been burdened by past interpretations and The Lie, and so children make and do whatever they want without judgment in innocence. This is why most children run around happy and excited in simplicity; they are full of the creative power of the universe, which has not yet been filtered or polluted by the surrounding psychological world. Children are unified with the power of life, just as adults should be. There is no reason why we should stop being creative and stop thinking of new things to bring about; it's our nature, by nature.

We should all have a creative pastime. And the more physical and mental effort involved in the pastime, the greater the results and conversion of mental and physical energy will be. In other words, the more intense and creative your pastime is, the greater the transformation will be for you. A mix of pastimes and creative expression is great as well. If you like to write, it is good to also get up and take a run or have some type of physical workout.

The more time you spend working out or being creative with your body and creating things beyond yourself, the more relief you will feel from mental burden. Another major thing to be aware of, as always, is that you, the creative force, is in charge of your intention, and if you are not aware, then The Lie and dysfunctional psychology will create for you. Instead of doing things out of enjoyment, The Lie can force you into depressing pastimes such as substance abuse, or even create miserable and violent scenarios.

COLLECTIVE PHYSICAL ACTION AND PHYSICAL CREATION

The way we create on an individual level projects into how we create as a whole. Much of what humanity has brought into the world is manifested through more than one individual and oftentimes through a significant duration of time. Civilizations and communities are built in joint effort, with a group mentality; this is the prime example of collective creation and the breakdown of culture. There are plenty of examples around today that show collective creation, and pop culture displays this very well. As a whole, people will sometimes physically create and express creativity by joining organizations or teams, following trends, and taking on new fads. In this, the creativity of the collective, whether it is of a media trend or some organization, reflects into the individuals who have taken on their new identities; they become a part of what has been collectively created. This can be displayed by major music trends, in which fans of a genre or type of music begin to dress, act, and even develop art and music similar to that of the major trend. This is how those individuals choose to express their creativity, and although it may not be completely original, it is often the only way in which people, especially younger generations, can release the creative energy within themselves. What is unique is that sometimes out of the collective trend, a new form of art or music will be born when a trend follower creates a variation of the original form. In some way, we all add our own variations to something already created, and we are supposed to. That is transformation.

However, collective trends, those trends that have already been created, can be dangerous and can actually destroy creativity. This is especially true when trend followers cease to be creative and start taking on the identity of the trend versus being a part of its furthered uniqueness and creativity. Remember that all things must change and energy transforms, so when people hold on to something, or don't allow something to change, there is conflict and combustion. This can be displayed by extremist groups, whether they are cultural or ideological, in which the definition of the group takes over, and its repetitive nature breeds conflict instead of uniqueness.

Creativity will always flow and transform, and it shows throughout collective periods in history. This is visible in the time span of the arts, sciences, and philosophies. There have always been major eras of arts, architecture, literature, philosophy, and music in which a variety of these forms were all interrelated and distinctively unique. During the Renaissance, which actually translates to rebirth, art, architecture, music, and philosophy were so diversified and original in their own sense that the creation of these new forms soared. For a span of about four hundred years, Western European society experienced an influx of amazing creativity and ingenuity in which artists such as Michelangelo and Da Vinci invented new forms of art and even technology. Mozart brought into the world the most renowned symphonies and music compositions, and scientists, including Sir Isaac Newton, came up with the most fundamental physical science principles. The Renaissance was literally an era of rebirth, and the intention of the universe was to bring about creative transformation to humankind. Prior to the Renaissance, Western Europe and the Roman Empire had fallen, and a period of crisis burdened much of the civilization. The turmoil from the fall and the past Roman national identity had suppressed any new creativity from arising, whether it was of cultural or artistic value. With the strong imperial grip out of the way and social struggle on the rise, a large portion of Europe fell to what was known as the Dark Ages. Soon after the Dark Ages the Renaissance arrived, and creativity made its way through the ashes of a fallen civilization and darkness. The Renaissance represents the nature of life and our individual creative existences, and it is regarded as one of the greatest transformational eras in history. It has a lesson to tell us: flow and transform. Humanity seems to hold to tightly to its creations instead of just continuing to create new forms and move with life. We must relinquish some of our attachment to what we have made and to our individual ideologies. This is the nature of existence; change and creativity that will always arise from the stagnancy of life. The underlying message behind all this: *Be the universe.*

Chapter Eight:
Being One with Creation, Being As the Universe

Being the Universe

Shakespeare's famous quote has a meaning far deeper than words. "To be, or not to be: that is the question," and that really is the question. The option is for us to be here, to be a part of the universe—to *be the universe*. On the other hand, the second option in Shakespeare's "question," which is not an option but a result of resistance to the first option, is not to be a part of the universe, not to be one with creation. When we stray from this fundamental principle, when we stray from being as the universe, we stop moving with the path of creation itself.

The universe is an expansive force, which is why it is considered infinite. The path it takes is an endless one, and its course is really just unlimited potential. What makes the universe endless, then, is that truly unimaginable potential for there to be anything at any given point. This means that at any point of the universe's chronological existence, even before the theoretical big bang beginning, there are endless possibilities for something to be created. Even when there is nothing there, just space, the universe is infinite because anything can form or happen within that space. This reflects directly into each of our individual selves because we are the universe and contain the access to execute endless possibilities.

The closest in words that we can ever get to understanding the universe and life is that the universe and life are here because they *are* the intention to bring life or existence about *from endless possibilities*. Look at it like this: all the stars just so happened to form from primary atomic elements, which gave way to the combustion and combination of other elements, which eventually formed planets from cosmic activity, which ended up in the orbit of a star, and one of those planets happened to develop an atmosphere and organic life. That planet is Earth. The possibility for planets like Earth to form life is always there, but not every planet develops life. Earth was a possibility, just as your birth was a possibility, and a number of scenarios could have prevented it, but somehow it still occurred. There was an intention beyond the human mental construct that *intended* Earth to be and *intended* you to be born.

Some may consider that intention to be God or a higher source, but the best way to understand it is that it just is. Regardless of belief, that intention formulates endless possibilities into existence; it is an infinite intelligence. Our existence, and all existence, is here to bring about diversity within the infinity of that intelligence, within the infinity of space. That is why there are forms, life and death, rise and fall. The physical universe *is* the brought about creativity beyond the theoretical expanding space which it considered to be. This is not about theology, cosmology, or any scientific ideal, this is the reality, existence from a creating factor, that which we have come to call the universe. It may be God to some, or science to others, but the fact is that it is beyond the personality of each individual person and each individual mind, and it is rooted within the very energy that allows you to be. We harness its capacity to execute our intentions into creation; this is displayed in our abilities to commit physical action and to physically create. This means that when you direct your intention, when you direct your potential to commit physical action, you have become the universe. By directing your intention, you become intention, and therefore you are the universe.

TRUE INTENTION THROUGH THE UNIVERSE

It is important to know that there is a major difference between true intention through the universe and distorted intention through your psychological state. We can say that The Lie is distorted intention through psychological state, being that The Lie is understandably out-of-control psychology, but what does it mean, exactly, to use true intention? Isn't true intention any intention put to action? The answer to that is both yes and no.

The yes stipulates that any intention, no matter what it is, becomes true intention when executed, even if it has risen out of a distorted psychological state. The reason goes into the fact that conflict is the universe's way of putting existence back on its continued course, so even distorted intentions put to action are here to display for us the examples of what happens when we lack true control over our intentions; they are a part of learning. Those distorted intentions cause conflict and pain, and it is just like the pain you feel when you get a cut. It is not pleasant because it is there to force you into awareness of the danger that is present. Distorted intention comes into action to show you the power of your intention. The realist view here is that the entire universe couldn't care less what you or anyone else does. It has its path, and it will keep expanding or reformulating, with or without you, and with or without the human race. The choice here is for us to open our eyes up to use true intention, to learn from the examples, so we can flow with the course of the universe. If our intentions become so distorted that they completely miss the purpose and intention of the universe, which is to embrace life and bring about creation in beautified diversity, then we will be knocked off the course of the universe as directors of this power.

As is the case with us, the universe is also learning in a sense, preparing a species such as humanity to see if we can handle our evolved minds and abilities. So we have an option: to wake up and become the universe, be and do what the universe does by using our true intention and creativity, or allow our distortions to prevent us from being the species that evolves to this level.

So what is true intention, then? True intention in the teachings of the Buddha describes right intention, an intention that does not create harm and is free of desire. It is an intention free from the ways of the world. The teachings of Jesus also describe this sense of intention, in which Christ states that he lives amongst the world and not in it, as I remember learning when I was a child in Bible school. So what is this idea of being free from the ways of the world? It simply means to continue with the course of life, or creation, not becoming lost in the impermanence of what is created, which is everything. Humanity becomes so entangled in the various things of this world that we have attached to them, holding on and doing all we can to prevent them from dying and changing. We attach to our stories, material objects, and even the personalities of ourselves and others, forgetting that these are all created forms and things, destined to transform. We forget the nature of the universe and the nature of creation. This is where desire comes in, which Buddha discussed greatly.

From what I have come to understand, desire is the psychology of trying to hold on to or hoard the things and experiences of the world. People desire material wealth, sex, drugs, other people for relationships and security, and status. All of these are temporary things, embodiments, or experiences, that will never be accessible every moment of every day, and so they are subject to change and transformation. Our distorted psychology and The Lie are the ways of the world, which are too impermanent. The only thing that is always there, that is always constant, as discussed, is the potential and intention for anything to be, as these are the unified powers that are life. Anything coming into existence arrives from the still moment in which its potential resides, and it is inevitably activated by the intent for it to be. This we can consider natural intention, or true intention, the intention that activates occurrences to bring new life.

To sum it up, true intention is intention that is free from The Lie, free from your psychological fears and wants. It is an intention not bound to any mental construct. It arises out of a state of peace, out of nothing, and it has no premeditated gain. It is the intention just to create, just to do so; an intention beyond selfishness, and an intention in uniqueness to benefit all. So when you use true intention, you are free from the idea of *"How is this going to make me better than everyone?"* You do not become warped by your own psychology demanding you to be greater by any definition; instead, you create out of the power of creation. Some creative actions may need to be taken for higher quality or life lifting purposes, such as a humanitarian change, but the minute a thought or idea has taken over to predetermine the goal of your intention, your intention has been taken over by that thought or idea. That intention is now no longer original. When our intentions lack originality we become stuck to things and experiences that have already been created. There is no progression and continuity, and that is what warps us. Most of our fears, emotions, and desires tend to be dragged-out feelings, and as such, they are unoriginal and unprogressive. They can severely pollute our intention. Along this line, we can say that true intention comes from originality.

ORIGINALITY

The word originality is derived from the word origin, which definitively means "where something or anything arises."[8] Originality itself is literally defined as something that is fresh, new, and original. So when we look at originality, we must realize that in order to be original, what we do must be original, and it must be fresh. What is the original, or foundation, to all of this then, specifically our intentions? The answer to that is yet another imperative repeat, a principle of this book, which is that originality is synonymous with the intention of the universe. So true intention and originality are one and the same, and they are present to bring about the new, to give rebirth from death, and to continue the transformational recycling of life. The origin of all things *is* intention, the intention for things to exist in the first place, and that intention is always original.

Both being unified, what we want to look at is how to *be* original. Essentially, to be original, we must always have fresh experiences, and all things must come about from the new and continually be transformed. To understand originality better, we can use the term "reborn." Just as we discussed the Renaissance, which translates to rebirth, we should continually be having a renaissance in all aspects of our own lives. In so doing, we become original, and we are true in intention. So how do we become reborn? The idea of rebirth implies that there must be death, and so there are intervals of death and rebirth in the processes of our originality. This means that in order to be original, we must go through the cycles of death and rebirth.

The next consideration is which aspects we go through in death and rebirth. The answer is all aspects. Death and rebirth should not just occur in your cellular or physical biology; it should occur in all things you do, think, and inhabit. The reason any conflict arises is because something is obstructing the natural course of life and death, and when something is not allowed to die out or is obstructed, conflict arrives as the traffic director. This is extremely obvious in the human world and in how we have used our minds and intention. We have not allowed the things we have created and idealized to die out, which they are supposed to do.

---

8   Webster's Dictionary and Thesaurus, "**Originality**,"1999.

By obstructing that path, we lose sight of intention, because intention is of an original nature which means it is meant to bring about change.

Most significant in all this is the obstruction that occurs within our own psychology, which has turned into the very lie that has distorted our abilities as a species. We pay no attention to the fact that most of our mental processes carry on long after the pertinent scenario to them has passed. We become stuck in them, especially our fears, anxieties, and wants, and they do not allow for fresh, new, and original ideas, thoughts, or concepts to come in. This is unoriginality. What we are thinking and doing has become so unoriginal that we are literally derailing ourselves from the path of universal intention.

So how do we become original; how do we prevent conflict for ourselves and others? It goes back to being a witness. The first step in any of this is to realize that all the processes discussed in this book are cycles, like birth and death. You will go from realizing and witnessing to putting your power to action—and back and forth, round and round. The only way to come back to originality, however, is to realize that which is unoriginal. From there, your actions can become original. This will continue in a natural cycle, and all you have to do is flow with it. All that you need to do to put yourself back on the track of progression, to become original, is to look at what is going on in your mind and be able to recognize the unoriginality in yourself. If you can catch yourself worrying about a situation that happened some time ago, something that has passed, you have caught unoriginality in play, and just by doing that, the death process of that particular experience or thing is allowed to begin. Most of the time when we see something we do not like in our thoughts or in action, we obstruct it even more by disliking it or trying to forget about it, and by doing that, we just focus on what is already unoriginal. The key here is to not obstruct it but just to realize the unoriginality and conflict-breeding nature of whatever it is that is occurring in these terms…let itself play out. Let your psychological unoriginality run out of fuel, or better yet, let it die out.

This has to relate to our emotions and opinions as well. Emotions and opinions tend to be extremely dragged-out feelings and thoughts. If you can catch yourself latching on to an emotion or irrelevant idea that has passed, even if it is seconds old, you have recognized the unoriginality of it. Originality is instantaneous and progresses only with continued creative intention. Emotions and opinions occur in an instant, but neither of them carries on with creative intention, unless of course they are directed to do so. Many artists and musicians direct their emotions and prolonged feelings into art or music. This is an example in which emotions can carry on with an original intention. They become fuel for a new created form, and in that, their prolongation serves a higher purpose—in the transformation of feeling into art. However, for most, emotions and opinions are an unoriginal and run-on occurrence blocking the rebirth of new experiences and ideas. They tend to be destructive deadweight for your journey through life. We have all, including myself, wasted hours thinking and being emotional over something that has long since passed, and there is nothing interesting or creative about it. It is a prevention of originality and a hindrance to creative living.

CREATIVE LIVING – DYING TO LIVE

The process for becoming original is one of patience; it requires your full attention and intention. This is the foundation for creative living, to be observant of all and to be still at times. To be true in intention, to live creatively, the death process in what we do must continually be in cycle; we can say that in order to creatively live, we must be dying to live. Death seems easy to understand: it is the cessation of a thing or an experience, the theoretical end of something that was, and the making of space for the new to arrive. It truly is simple, but arriving to it is difficult. To be original, we already know that what is unoriginal must be recognized and allowed to wither away; observation must be there. That is the hard part, for death *is* a process of patience. Birth is generally instantaneous, just like the start of anything, but death is progression. It takes the movement of time for death to be completed into the transformation of something else. For that movement to continue freely there must be patience. This means that we must be patient with all things that die out, including our experiences, thoughts, ideas and creations, and ultimately ourselves and others.

But how is dying living? How do you become patient with this process? The answer to that is to let death take its course in all things that we do—and all existing things. There is no doubt that it is not as easy as it sounds, and the only reason is because we are used to our psychological attachment to things, to what we have created, and to the ideas and images of who we are. Arriving at the conclusion that nothing is permanent and silently allowing all things to die out without obstruction is the challenging part of all creation and life. It is that undisturbed watching, the observation of what comes around and what leaves, that tends to be left unpracticed. We are so full of thoughts and potentials that we forget to be observant of the processes of life and death. That process of silent observation, of patience, is also learning. By observing death instead of trying to stop it, or run from it, we become patient with it, inevitably allowing originality to come forth. This is also the nature of true intention, and why originality arises from the unobstructed power of death. True intention comes from nothing, from nowhere. It happens because it is to bring about something from nothing. A potential unfolds from nothing—where else would it come from? You cannot build another building on top of a building, at least without there being some form of destruction first to create space, and you cannot have new life or something arise without the death of something. That is what death is, the withering away into nothing, which eventually leads to something. Death is the process into nothing, and so death is a power from which life arises.

I remember that as a child, I would often pretend to be dead when many things began to bother me. I would lie on the floor or in the bed and act as if I had just died. I now realize just how much of a spiritual practice that was—and what I was doing. I was allowing my entire psyche to die temporarily from the thoughts, ideas, and issues concerning me, pretending I was nonexistent. I was creating space from the death of what I was feeling and allowing the moment of peace, the moment of nothing, to arise so I could get up and be happy again. Little did I realize that at six years old, I had figured out a secret to life: by allowing myself to die temporarily, I was allowing the experiences and thoughts in my head to die as well. I became unified and observant with the temporary experience of my own "death," and I was practicing dying to live.

What I remember in even greater detail as a child was how I would stare at the ceiling for hours, wondering what it would be like if I weren't me, if I did not exist. One night, I went so far into the thought that I forgot for several moments that I was me. I had imagined not being me so deeply that I had become briefly stuck in a state of nonexistence. It was scary considering that I was a child. It was as if I had left my life behind, and I snapped out of it quickly. I now realize that what I had done was a step further than pretending I was dead; I'd gone directly into the curiosity and ultimate fear of my death; I went into the abyss of nonexistence and became one with death for several seconds.

CREATIVE LIVING – FROM THE ABYSS

The idea of the abyss and its meaning are rooted from ancient cosmogony in which the term describes an immeasurable space and the primal chaos before creation.[9] The idea of the abyss can be considered the ancient mystical term for what science today calls the infinity of space. The abyss touches on a level that we cannot understand, and the term is not meant in any way to give us an ultimate answer to the how of infinity, nor is it meant to explain how everything got here. It simply is telling us this is the unknown; leave it that way, unless you can venture into it.

For a brief few seconds as a child, I had, and it is unexplainable. I only remember going into the abyss because it was a feeling that I can describe as not really a feeling—it was the feeling of *me* not being *myself.* At that time, it was extremely scary for me to explore. I now realize today why the abyss is defined as it is, as a primal chaos before creation, as endless. The feeling I had felt of not feeling, of not being me, and of being suspended in a seemingly endless state, was chaos to my mind. I could not mentally comprehend nonexistence, so when I snapped out of it, I felt as if I'd gone into and come out of chaos. The irony was that the "chaos" I had gone into was actually peace. It was the peace that comes after the death of something, like the peace after all the trees have died in the start of winter and the landscape is still with snow. Yet I had not realized it until years later, when peace became a necessity in my life.

That primal chaos before creation we can now redefine here as the primal *peace* before creation. It is the deadness from which something comes into existence. That is exactly where creation comes from, the abyss. Why else would there be creation, because in the first place, there was the abyss or the nothing where creation was not, and from there creation became.

9   Dictionary.Com, "**Abyss**" (3a), http://dictionary.reference.com/browse/abyss, (accessed 12/6/2010)

Whatever we choose to call that beginning is up to us; however, we should understand it for one thing: from stillness and peace arises the power of creation. In reality, we should be going into and coming out of the abyss in a cycle, which is birth and death. When we allow ourselves to die temporarily from an experience, we go into the abyss. When we take a deep breath or when we become still to examine something, we go into the abyss. When anything dies, it goes back into the abyss.

In another sense, the abyss is rest. Peace is rest, stillness and patience are rest, and death is rest. When you are at peace, or are patient with the comings and goings of life, the power of creation that is in you, and that you are, is at rest. This means you are active only when the power of creation in you is ready, when the power of creation arises from what it is, peace and limitless potential.

WAKING FROM THE SLUMBER: THE POWER STRUGGLE

In order for there to be the movement of life, rest is necessary. The power that powers all life ignites itself from that point of rest; it goes into and out of slumber. It is primary; things must have been still, and must stop, in order to have formed and reformed. There must be those breaks of rest, of stillness, in order for life to continue on the path of creativity and originality. The principles of the universe are the same as in your individual life. When you go to work, you are given a break; you are allowed to rest to regain vitality. The same goes for everything else that exists, and there are periods of rest in order for the original to arise again. Most people have the concept that rest occurs during the sleep state, which it significantly does, but rest should occur not only when the body has biologically shut down. When awake and conscious, there should be intervals of rest, intervals in which we allow ourselves to die temporarily to moments of peace and relaxation. As often as we can, we should stop and observe our surroundings, breathing in the air around us. Take several moments to allow yourself to die into the observation or sensation of something. Maybe even take a seat and drink some tea, and while doing so, you are resting your mind even though your body is in motion. This allows the power of creation within you, the power that is you, to go into its slumber, and when ready, it will awaken in you again.

If you write, as I have found writing this book, you will find moments when you can no longer write, and you must take a break. I have taken many periods of rest in writing this book, and at times, my creative abilities went into slumber. Some days I did not write at all. I could not force out the creative power that allowed me to do so, and so I let it rest. Rest applies to all forms of action as well, all forms of movement through which you live. Breaks, periods of silence, and simple experiences of sensing, such as observing a forest or listening to water, are adequate for the balance of creative living movement. All aspects of moving life, and all aspects of physical action in relation to us, must go back into the abyss of rest.

We can look at it as a charging mechanism for originality and refreshment. Our physical bodies must sleep so we can be recharged for physical exertion. During the day, however, many people forget that our physical interpretational abilities need rest, and our physical creative abilities need rest as well. There should be periods in which the mind ceases from physically interpreting what we are experiencing—and periods in which there is no action from those experiences. What this means is that we should take in an experience without having it physically interpreted, by just observing it without the response of physical action or thought. We can call this exploration or allowing yourself to journey. I often find myself getting in a car and driving to a far place I have not seen before, just to experience it without thinking. My body may be in action, but I am allowing my creative power and my mind to go to rest by just observing and driving, without thinking too much about what is going on. I find that getting away stops the action of thought for a brief period because the body's sensing and observing action is put into play. I enjoy journeying from time to time, even occasionally going to a park to "stop and smell the roses," as the wise saying goes.

The case for much of humanity is that we have not allowed rest to occur in our action, in our power. Instead, we do not want to accept rest; we want to keep on going with a particular action, not allowing it to die out. It may be time for a break, but instead we need to gain more, or do more, or get somewhere. We invent one thing and then try a million more times to enhance it, adding a million more concepts to whatever we are doing, not giving our physical creative abilities a break. We put ourselves in overdrive, revving the engine of creativity, and it responds with distress. We are wasting energy in the nightmare we have created, in our psychology, versus letting rest occur and eventually allowing creativity to arise out of slumber. How so? By attempting to gain everything we can, by attempting to overpower others, by becoming obsessed with the things in life. By trying so hard to make something of ourselves, we are attempting to escape the slumber of power. We want to know where our power has gone when it is at rest, and we think to ourselves, *Well, if I am not doing anything, then what is the purpose of this moment?* Or, *I can't live like this; I need to make something of myself.* These are just a couple of the thoughts that run through our minds when we cannot feel that moving power in the moment. The truth is that you can do nothing if you do not feel as if the power in you is in motion. All you can do is allow it to rest. When *it* is ready, *it* will arise. The more you try to force power, the more you try to become something or gain something to be powerful, the further you will force power away because you are not allowing it to rest.

Humanity has been doing this for thousands of years; it is called the power struggle. We attempt to gain power through all kinds of hellish means, and in the end, no one is satisfied. This is because the power struggle is an illusion, and you cannot gain power through force, contrary to popular belief. If you look around, you'll see that true creativity and art amongst most is dwindling, and that is because as a whole, humanity has wasted its energy in the power struggle, in the attempt to be something, versus accepting that power must rest and it will not always be accessible every second. That *is* our problem: we expect the universe to shoot power through us nonstop, but it does not work like that. It is like an electric appliance. If you leave the power on too long or all the power is directed into one, it will overload or shut down. Power has to be shared amongst many appliances or shut down at times. We are enduring that trouble, forcing ourselves and our power into a deeper sleep by wasting what energy we have in the nightmare in trying to get out. Let it be, as the Beetle's song goes. It is the only thing you, and all of us, can do, and when the time comes, true power, the power of creation, will flow. You don't force yourself to become a true artist or musician—it is already there, and it is a matter of how you space your life in order for it to come through. If you feel the music or art within you, you allow it to come out when it is ready. The same goes for any creative act. The summary is that creation is always there, but it must arise from patience and rest.

In writing, the more you try to force out ideas, the deeper you become stuck in writer's block. Sometimes you just have to get up and walk away, go and rest. There is nothing you can do about it. Both your mind, and the power that comes through your mind, must rest. When humanity recognizes the insanity as a whole and takes a break from all the psychological unrest, creativity will rise. Relating to the Renaissance again, humanity went into a deep sleep during the Dark Ages, and when it was time, the power of creativity jumped into action throughout Europe for several hundred years. Instead of letting this be an unstable cycle, we should all allow the constructs of our minds, and of our world, to die out naturally. In letting all things die, from our thoughts to the things in our lives, true power will not be blocked and will awaken from its slumber.

YOU

All this boils down to one point: you. It is through you, and every human, that power flows and can flow. If you are not awakened to the reality of true power, it will simply stay in rest and come out somewhere else, somehow. Because we are the medium, the transformers of the energy current of life, we can overload or even cause resistance to the power flowing through us. We can malfunction, blocking the current of universal power from its path. What gives us life, what we can consider a spiritual or metaphysical side of us, is also this power. We are that power of the universe, and at the same time, the converter box through which that power runs. This should humble us and give us humility to realize that the physical life we endure is a medium for this much deeper power that motivates all life. That power is *the power of creation*, which arises from the intelligence of infinity. It is here to mastermind the show of life throughout our universe; it is here to put its power into all things that unfold in it. Define it as you would like, but science, God, metaphysics, philosophy, and every other form of human interpretation and understanding are here to help us recognize this power and embrace it. I have chosen not to lean to a specific stance or name in this book on that creative power because I do not wish to give a mental position to a power that I want you to feel, and not just idealize.

When you put to action your creative power, you will feel that truth, and it just is. You may run, play a sport, produce music, or invent or build something. In whatever creative act you do, whether you do it for enjoyment, as a hobby, or for the sheer act of just being able to do it, you have come to experience the power of creation within you. You have derived happiness from the root of life because you have become the force of life, a force engaged in whatever creative act you undergo.

There are many aspects and views to the power and mind-set that I have written about in this book, and they all point to show you how you work, and how this power inside you works. One transition is necessary; one step into this power is all it takes. If it hasn't already happened, hopefully it soon will, especially after an effort to read this material. That transition is this: realizing that you are the biggest influential power on yourself. You are the power that can get up and run, or paint, or write. You are the power that can pick up any book you choose, read it, and store it in your mind however you wish. You are the power that interprets all the situations you encounter—and the powerhouse that can intake whatever type of energy, negative or positive, and spit it back out however you choose. Most of all, you are the power that can go in and out of death. You can let your experiences and past interpretations die out, bringing them back to life when you want. At any time, you can enter your own memory and experience the past through it—or you can go directly into the sense of a new experience. You are the universe experiencing yourself; you are the power and we are all the power. When this is clearly understood, all of us—you and everyone else who wakes up to realize this—will become the writers of the new chapters of life, and we will all continue this book …

Ten Lies & Ten Truths

A Follow Up-
Everyday Reminders for
Empowerment-

TEN LIES

Lie I.

The number one lie of The Lie is that you are not enough. As was discussed multiple times throughout the book the idea that you do not amount to something or you do not meet up to a special definition is a killer to your experiences in life. It is a deeply rooted psychological fear, and can create much conflict for you.

Realize that:

You are always enough because you get to experience life, how can you be anything more than life when life really is everything?

In every moment you are wherever you are and are doing whatever you are doing. You truly cannot meet up to anything other than whatever you are being in the moment, and the moment of experience is greater than any definition in your head.

Definitions, standards, and what you can be classified as are only ideas created from our thoughts, you can meet up to them if you choose, but ultimately they are just thoughts and ideas.

Lie II.

Another common lie of The Lie is that things will bring you contentment. Although things can assist you in your journey through life, and they are interesting, they cannot make you content. After all things are here just for you to experience and are here to assist you, they are not permanent, and so cannot bring you the eternal joy of life and creativity.

Realize that:

The more you try to find yourself in material things, the further from content you will be. Your struggle to be more through material things or your attachment to the impermanent material world will only take you away from realizing you are here to enjoy the art of life.

Wanting can become a major psychological disease and an addiction. Mentally the reason we can compulsively want things is so we can fulfill something set in our minds, which is illusory. You are already everything you need to be, once again which is life, so live.

Lie III.

It was discussed in the book how thoughts and ideas have energy, and so energy can transfer into you. Remember that the energy of The Lie can come into you if you are not watching, and so if you are around negative thoughts, or negative actions, they can take you over. Forgetting that The Lie can take you over is The Lie.

Realize that:

When around negative occurrences, know that The Lie or negative energy is there, and do your best not to react to it. In some cases this may mean walking away briefly from somebody, taking a walk alone, or leaving completely from a scenario.

LIE IV.

The Lie that you are not good enough in the eyes of others is insanity. Remember that this lie is only a reflection of someone else's ideas. Although this was discussed briefly, human relationships should not be set to a wanting standard or special definition. Do not allow this lie to take you over, if someone else feels you are not enough, they are themselves caught in The Lie and are not in control. You will only be arguing with someone else's idea, or trying to meet up to someone else's idea and that is no different than arguing with writing on paper. So when you are confronted with this, let it be, walk away and realize that you are the power of creation, and what does some idea matter to that.

Realize that:

You are already what you need to be!

LIE V.

This was not discussed in the book but blaming is also The Lie. Blame is an idea and a thought, and when you blame your latching onto an idea of something to make you feel better. Other's may not be right for their actions, but to be controlled by blaming, and the idea of blame, is to just become possessed by another idea and no problem will be solved there, just increased stress and insane thinking.

Realize that:

Blame is more self centered than creative, and disconnects you from life. The more you blame, the longer the negative idea or problem remains stuck in *your* mind.

If you find it hard to be around somebody or something that was a "problem," you may have to break contact. It is better to break contact with the person or scenario which is problematic, sticking around may fuel your ideas and thoughts of blame and inflame your conflict. Breaking contact will allow for rest and peace to come in and inevitably for the conflict and blame to dissolve.

Lie VI.

This was also not discussed in too much detail in the book, but arrogance, extreme pride, and self-centered mentality are also The Lie. When you think you are better than somebody else, or are only concerned with yourself in a scenario, you are caught in the idea that you are better and more important than everything else, which is The Lie. You forget that creation is everything, that you are creation, and that you are a part of everything else created. You really detach yourself from true power at that point.

Realize that:

You share the same life force and creativity as every other form of life: *be one with everyone and everything else, and you will be the universe.* It does not get greater than that.

LIE VII.

Along with arrogance and blame comes judgment of others and life. When you judge others you give them a label and definition, and we all know that being stuck in defining and standardizing causes conflict. Same goes with life. Instead of judging, accept whatever and whoever comes your way, ultimately everything will pass so you are only wasting time excessively defining, labeling, and judging everything.

Realize that:

The universe, space, and nature have no opinion on life. Ask a tree, a field, an asteroid, a planet or a lake what they think about a scenario between you and somebody, and see your response. You will get silence, which is the best, it is no judgment, and it causes no conflict.

It doesn't matter how different, or how unacceptable someone else is to you, they are also a part of creation and in the greatest aspect are also a part of the one life. They may not meet up to certain ideas, but does that really matter? Once again those are just ideas, so don't become possessed by them. When you judge others, you are being controlled by a thought, idea, or broken down even a fear. If you cannot get along with someone, stay away so at least the idea and judgment does not have ease to start. This may be very hard at times.

Lie VIII.

Forgetting the purpose of the past is The Lie. When you become trapped in thinking about or become extremely emotional about the past, you forget that the past is here for you to learn from, and you disregard its purpose, which is to help you out. Learning from past experiences, such as from something that hurts you, or something that shows you what works and what does not, helps you build a better present and future.

Realize that:

The past is gone, and it is left as an idea or thought in your memory, so use the ideas like ideas in a book and learn from them.

Lie IX.

Forgetting that you have intention over your own actions and words is The Lie. When you forget that you choose how to talk and act, The Lie is in control of you, and anxiety, anger, pain, or psychological fear can be the director of your words and actions.

Realize that:

The power that you have intention over yourself is true freedom and true empowerment. It is greater than silver and gold, and who knows it may bring you those.

Lie X.

Thinking that the future will heal all your problems, or waiting for the future to bring you some peace is also The Lie. Remaining in a problematic scenario saying *"I'll just be here for a little bit more, and then everything will be fine* or *tomorrow everything will be better when this or that happens"* is insanity. There is an idea or definition in your head keeping you stuck to a problem because the idea doesn't want to die. This goes for gut instincts. Don't anticipate something in hopes it can do something for you, or don't think about something if you feel you should do something else.

Realize that:

Time to take true action is always there, because intention is always there.
The future itself is an idea or blueprint in your mind of what can happen, it happens however it happens by multiple factors, so to be stuck on the future is no different than staring at drawn out blueprints to a possible home for a decade, and forgetting about everything else.

TEN TRUTHS

TRUTH I.

The truth of all truths is that the truth and true power are accessible anywhere at any time; the truth is always in you. You are the truth because you are creativity and can use that very same power. You can access creation at anytime even by perceiving it, and mostly by putting it to action, by creating something and also when watching the creation in the world around you. This truth is that truth is always present.

Realize that:

At any moment you can do anything. You can draw a picture, plant a garden, write a book, leave and go somewhere, move away, create a conversation, listen to the water, practice breathing meditation, you can do anything, and you can experience anything in this life. The only thing that produces our creations and our experiences to be bad or negative is our minds and our thoughts. Only *your* mind in the end can stop you from being free and creating freely.

TRUTH II.

As well as realizing that the truth is in you, the fact is that truth exists in everyone and everything you interact with, and that if you are truthful and aware of your intentions with others and with life, then the truth in you will reflect in others.

Realize that:

When you choose to go beyond The Lie, and see the truth in all of life, you will become that truth. Respecting other life forms and other people will only bring you respect: remember that truth activates truth. Give truth and respect to others, give love, and you will receive it, just as we learned as children.

TRUTH III.

Another major truth to remember is the truth that what goes into you affects you. This is not just on a physical level, but on a mental level as well. Thoughts and ideas can enter exterior to you and influence you. Thoughts, like streams, can flow through you, and a polluted stream, or polluted thought can corrupt you. It can come from anywhere, from what you hear and what you see.

Realize that:

The information you choose to ingest has a direct affect on you. The more negative ideas you put in, the more negative ideas will come out. Unless you view information without opinion or judgment, information that seems to be bad to you will create the feelings and thoughts of bad inside of you and you may not even be aware of it.

Many thoughts and ideas are unoriginal, and not from you. There have been ideas and a variety of mentalities that have been passed down for centuries from generation to generation. Original thought comes either when you are creative, when you are using an old idea to formulate a new idea, or when you are completely in the moment and aware of what is happening and of what you're thinking.

TRUTH IV.

A great truth that many of us forget is that everything transforms and changes. We often become trapped by events and things, and ourselves, and we forget that all things, including ourselves, change. We must transform, and the more often this is realized, the easier our transformations and changes will be. In fact it is up to us to transform ourselves.

Realize that:

We are transformers of the energy in and around us. You can take your thoughts, and transform your mental energy into art or writing. You can take materials from this world, and transform them into your creations. You are a transformational being, remember that always.

TRUTH V.

Along with understanding transformation, another major truth to remember is that how you physically act is a means for the direct physical transformation in your body. Being involved in some physical activity or taking a walk everyday through a park is a great means to change how you physically feel.

Realize that:

You have a physical body to experience this life, and by all means do your best to experience and put your body to action in whatever way you can. If work-outs and gyms are not your choice, maybe something peaceful like hiking will help you physically put your body to action.

Physically exerting energy from your body releases negativity that builds up, and it is a great way to release stress.

TRUTH VI.

The truth that what you speak has power should always be remembered. How you talk to others and the intentions of your words will display if you are truthful and in power, or if you are possessed by The Lie and negativity.

Realize that:

Complaining, insulting, and being negative in any means are not using your words with true power and intention. If you insult or talk down about others, you are only allowing yourself to become possessed by negativity, and giving away your intention to be a true human being.

Giving positive advice, constructive ideas, and complements out of sincerity are truthful in this sense. Even telling jokes to lighten the atmosphere in a negative scenario is considerably helping to clear away hostility, as long as the jokes are not provocative.

TRUTH VII.

Considering that you have the power to transform and power over your words, remember the truth that you *are* the change. The Gandhi quote, "be the change," points directly to this. It is the same as directing your intention and it applies to scenarios you find yourself in, such as when it may be necessary to make a move, or pursue something new, so bottom line truth: *be the change.*

Realize that:

Change happens no matter what; however there are fewer burdens when you consciously are the change in a scenario, especially if the scenario is allowing madness to take you over.

Sitting around thinking about changing, or talking about it, is cheap. If a change needs to be made for a more enlightened purpose, do so.

Truth VIII.

This was a primary truth discussed about The Lie, and that is that being an observer and a watcher of what is going on inside and outside of you is being the truth. When you choose to be directly observant of your mental and emotional state, along with observing the state of things around you, you come to a state of total realization where true action can happen.

Realize that:

Understanding and watching how your thoughts affect you, and watching the insanity of emotional conflicts around you allows you to step out of these cycles of madness. Your realization will inevitably allow you to *be the change,* as we discussed.

Truth IX.

In relevance to creativity, remember this truth: you can put your thoughts to work, or they can put you to work. You can use your ideas, definitions, what you are feeling, and anything else you are thinking to create visual artwork, music, writing, designs, philosophy, and so on. That is the truest purpose of thoughts, to be used as a means for the power of creation.

Realize that:

If there is a lot on your mind, use it to be creative. Write about your understandings or write about your experiences. If you can make music, or can attempt to draw or depict some form of art, do so. If you have a hobby, and there is a lot on your mind, get into your hobby: you will be putting your mind to work. If anything take a walk or a run, and put yourself into direct physical exertion. Use your power.

Truth X.

I will leave you with this final summary and truth: *You cannot win a race that is not a race, and life is not a race; it is an art, so treat it as so.* When you realize this truth all the beauty around you can unfold. Everything here is a part of the artwork which is life; it is a process of the patience and peace of creativity. Stillness and space are vital in the aspects of creation, because artwork itself is not a race; it is an act of majestic power. When you become patient with life, you can allow for the artwork of life to reformulate through you. Creativity arises from the silence, from the abyss, and when you treat yourself, others and life as you would treat the production of your own art, with patience and care, your life too becomes a masterpiece.

Realize that:

Anything you do or make is an art. Do what you enjoy, or at least do your best to treat what you are doing as an art. This applies to all aspects of your life: how you speak, how you write, how you act, how you relate to others, even how you move and how you perceive the world are an art. In any act you do there is the formulation of something; and that is creativity. See how life is when you treat your conversations, relationships, and actions period as so. Life *is* art; Life *is* creation.

ACKNOWLEDGMENTS

This page is a credit to all the spiritual teachers, educational teachers, and others who have shared with me their understandings, experiences, and wisdom. It comes from all the spiritual books I have read, all the martial arts classes and philosophies I have taken, some of the college courses I have taken relating to social science and psychology, and the interactions I have had with close friends. All my experiences and learning led me to come up with my own art, which is this book, to be a guide unto others. I thank all of you, teachers, guides, and friends alike, for being one with me, and this book is my expression of the oneness I have with you and the oneness I have with everyone and everything. We are all the power of the universe, and I am thankful for that creativity of life. May we all be pointers to truth, and may we all realize our connection.